our stories
are our survival

our stories are our survival

Lawrence Bamblett

Aboriginal Studies Press

First published in 2013
by Aboriginal Studies Press

© Lawrence Bamblett 2013

All rights reserved. No part of this book may be reproduced or transmitted in any form or by any means, electronic or mechanical, including photocopying, recording or by any information storage and retrieval system, without prior permission in writing from the publisher. The Australian *Copyright Act 1968* (the Act) allows a maximum of one chapter or 10 per cent of this book, whichever is the greater, to be photocopied by any educational institution for its education purposes provided that the educational institution (or body that administers it) has given a remuneration notice to Copyright Agency Limited (CAL) under the Act.

Aboriginal Studies Press
is the publishing arm of the
Australian Institute of Aboriginal
and Torres Strait Islander Studies.
GPO Box 553, Canberra, ACT 2601
Phone: (61 2) 6246 1183
Fax: (61 2) 6261 4288
Email: asp@aiatsis.gov.au
Web: www.aiatsis.gov.au/asp/about.html

National Library of Australia Cataloguing-in-Publication entry
    Author: Bamblett, Lawrence
    Title: Our stories are our survival/Lawrence Bamblett
    ISBN: 9781922059222 (pbk.)
    ISBN: 9781922059239 (ebook: pdf)
    ISBN: 9781922059246 (ebook: epub)
    ISBN: 9781922059253 (ebook: Kindle)
    Notes: Includes bibliographical references and index.
    Subjects: Wiradjuri (Australian people). Aboriginal Australians. Sports.
    Dewey Number: 994.0049915

Printed in Australia by Opus Print Group

Front cover: Wiradjuri country, photograph by Rachel Ippoliti.
Back cover: The Erambie Allblacks (author's collection).

Cover design by Greg Nelson, Upside Creative
Text design and typesetting by Greg Nelson, Upside Creative

Aboriginal and Torres Strait Islander people are advised that this publication contains names and images of people who have passed away.

This project has been assisted by the Australian Government through the Australia Council, its arts funding and advisory body.

One yard = 0.9144 metres
One Australian pound (currency) = $AUD1
One Australian shilling (currency) = 10 cents
Five bob = 5 shillings
Currency not adjusted to today's value.

June Murray sharing stories at Erambie, July 2011. (Author's collection)

Dedication

Erambie people are fearless, loud and generous. This book is dedicated to one of them. I only know my grandmother, Rebecca Bamblett, through the oral history of our community. I have been told: 'Your Grandmother would die at anyone's feet. She was never afraid of anyone.' I am thankful that my grandmother's generation possessed the strength, not only to resist unwelcomed intrusions on their lives, but to carry on our ways as they lived them. This book is for my Nan, she sounds like my kind of person.

Contents

Dedication vi

Illustrations viii

Acknowledgments ix

Introduction: The Storyteller 1

1 Straight-line stories 11

2 Telling stories: People and places 37

3 The famous Erambie Allblacks 63

4 Fighting at the gates 101

5 The Wiradjuri clever men 123

6 Representation: Words and people 161

7 Telling Australian stories 175

Notes 189

Bibliography 191

Index 199

Illustrations

(Between pp. 86–87)

Note about the figures: Most of the photographs sourced by the author are old. Although they are treasured possessions, they are scanned copies of a long gone original where no negatives are available. There is some degree of wear and tear.

Figure 1: Erambie Allblacks

Figure 2: The 'famous Cowra All Blacks'

Figure 3: Barnstorming Erambie Allblacks, 1929

Figure 4: Erambie junior team, the 'Baby Blacks', 1937

Figure 5: The railway gates

Figure 6: Harry Murray senior

Figure 7: Doolan Murray

Figure 8: Jim Murray at 13

Figure 9: Jim Murray, the 'Black Prince'

Acknowledgments

I am grateful to the people of Erambie. They have all contributed to this book in some way. Without the constant support and efforts of my parents, Mavis and Brian, my sister Caroline, Millie and Sylvia Ingram, Josie Ingram, June and Margaret Murray, the extraordinarily talented Jean and Joyce Merritt, as well as two of my idols Jim Murray and Roy Carroll, this book would not have been possible. They taught me about Wiradjuri excellence. I hope the stories I tell will in some small way ensure that they will never be forgotten. Some of the documentary research about Erambie was completed during my studies at Charles Sturt University. I thank the staff there for supporting my work. This book was written during a research fellowship at the Australian Institute of Aboriginal and Torres Strait Islander Studies (AIATSIS). I am grateful to AIATSIS for its commitment to community engagement and for supporting my unconventional approach to an academic research fellowship.

I want to thank the people who critically read the manuscript. Thanks to Rhonda Black and Rachel Ippoliti at Aboriginal Studies Press for their encouragement and support. Thanks to the judges of the Stanner Award for their kind words. The book is better thanks to Margaret McDonell's input.

Finally, my family, Beatrice and the little people, indulge my single-minded obsession with the history of Erambie. I thank them for their patience.

Introduction:

The Storyteller

By the fires, the Old Men told the tales
which held their listeners spell-bound.
(Ingamells 1951: 175)

Kooris come back to this place all the time. The older people talk about it. Whenever someone returns to live at Erambie they typically explain it by the saying, 'once you drink from the Lachlan River, where the snakes grow bigger, you always come back to the Lachlan River'. But he was different from all the others who come home. He re-energised an ancient oral history tradition.

It was the mid 1980s when he packed up and came home to live at Erambie. I first noticed he was home when I found an impressive motorcar and caravan in the community park near the entrance to the mission. A closer look revealed a campsite where he moved about, stoked a fire, and prepared a cup of tea. He was a big white-haired man with enormous fists and forearms. He wore the white cowboy hat, a plain white western shirt, blue jeans with a belt buckle and riding boots familiar to him from his days as a drover. 'G'day mate,' he said, with a hold on the 'may' in 'mate' that lasted a while and showed that he meant it. I smiled without replying and hung around his camp and watched him go about his daily routine. He sang to himself, mostly in English, as he worked, but when he noticed I was watching he sang using Koori words. 'Uncle Geebung used to talk in the lingo,' he recalled, 'when the manager wasn't around.' 'Aw, g'day mate, how ya been?' he said, and I looked up to see a visitor had come over from the mission. He gave his mate's hand a shake and they sat down for a drink of tea and a yarn. That was the first day I remember watching the Storyteller.

As I listened to the two old mates tell tales of what they'd been up to, I went through what I knew about him in my head. I knew he had been a professional boxer who fought in boxing tents and that he had seen his name in lights at the famous Sydney Stadium. People on the mission said that he was the first registered Koori boxing trainer and that he once owned a gym in Sydney. They reckoned he trained the champion Tony Mundine, and I had heard that his nephew and son were champion fighters. I knew that he worked for Koori organisations in Sydney because I heard Mum talking about it. Now I knew that he was retiring to Erambie because he told his mate, who replied, 'I heard you was coming home'.

It wasn't long before he moved into a tidy little house at the back of the mission. As he settled back into life there he encouraged people to share their stories. He was always saying that he grew up on Erambie when games, music and storytelling were 'the only entertainment on the mission'. His daily routine was scheduled around visits with other residents. They yarned for hours and drank tea. His company was anticipated and I often heard people say, 'he'll be along for a yarn in a minute'. Sometimes he rode his horse Champ but usually he marched, shadow boxing around the mission with a high step, whistling and singing a tune as he looked for a mate to have a yarn with. When he approached our house he would call out, 'ya there mate?' and he invited us to 'sit out here with me and have a yarn'. His yarns were more performance than conversation. Still, in me he always found a willing mate. He was a charismatic and skilful spinner of yarns who had a gift for storytelling.

He told a detailed and highly entertaining yarn about elders and life for Koori people on and off government reserves and missions. He usually started with an elongated, 'aww mate, I remember...'. He built anticipation in the story using his voice and body movements to the point where he would stand and mimic distinguishing vocal and physical features of the characters he brought to life before my eyes. Every so often he would ask, 'now you with me mate, you with me?' and when I acknowledged that I was he continued, 'aww mate, I remember...'. He sought a reaction and when he got one he became more animated and engaged in his performance.

When in the company of his peers he fed off their agreement with the truth of his account, repeatedly asking, 'now am I right sis? Am I right mate? You were there, ya with me?' He good-naturedly coaxed them to share their stories, 'come on now sis, come on brother, we gotta teach these young ones what we know'. He asked questions and directed the conversation to include discussion of the past. He delighted in their laughter when he mimicked a peculiar mannerism of a character in his story. His ability to imitate was fundamental to his storytelling style and he used it to great effect. During his performance he often smiled, shut his eyes and sighed, and it was as if he had returned to the past. And I felt like I was there with him.

Suddenly he would remember a detail, become excited. His eyes would open and he'd jump and laugh and congratulate himself for remembering, and his face would light up. The excitement would build in the story until he made his point and then he'd laugh and finish with, 'there you see mate, I remember, aww, do I what!' He'd barely finish his story as he'd march up the road, laughing and calling to see if his next mate was home.

There were other charismatic storytellers. Erambie was blessed with people who were gifted in the art. Two of my other favourites were a pair of beautiful sisters who came from a family of storytellers. They shared with their peers the ability to create vivid pictures with words. Beyond that, they were blessed with genius comedic timing that made them a joy to be around. They found humour in any event, no matter how serious. They giggled constantly as they took up endless invitations to share their stories. I found them very entertaining and enjoyed their company and the stories they told.

The warmth, caring nature and sense of humour of the senior men and women I grew up with at Erambie drew me in and I loved to sit all day with them and share their stories.

At the end of a typical day with them, my face would ache from smiling and my head would be filled with pictures of important people, places and events. Important enough to the people of Erambie that stories are told about them. Over time I learned the yarns well enough to be able to retell them. One day I told my mates about the place up the back of the mission — the railway gates — where I heard that fights used to be held. I mentioned names and certain fights I heard about as we walked the dirt track to the railway gates for a look.

I returned to a stable home with parents who live by and preach the virtues of the hard-working Koori men and women they know. My blessings include growing up in this nurturing, tight-knit community. Education was central to everyday life in my parents' home. However, neither of them demonstrated particular interest in, nor placed much value on, mainstream schooling. Some of the teachers I met in schools were excellent but I never felt comfortable in classrooms and I dropped out of high school at sixteen. My decision went unchallenged other than my mother asking, 'no more school?'

In place of school, I rose before dawn to join Erambie's seasonal workers. My days with them started with cups of tea; they lit and smoked cigarettes and prepared tools and lunches for the day ahead. They delighted in a patterned type of yarn where community gossip was reported before the previous day's conversations resumed. Once at work they yarned, joked and sang songs all day. A number of conversations took place at one time and all were required to keep up or be chastised. In the course of many conversations, I heard about their experiences of life. These were joyful and inspiring times.

Where these stories take me

My fascination with the social and cultural history of Erambie Mission is grounded in the community's oral history tradition. I watched the Storyteller and his peers bring to life the achievements of our community's storied athletes and leaders. My interest grew over time and as an adult I still gravitate toward the knowledgeable senior men and women from Erambie and I continue to seek their company. It is not uncommon that I sit with them all day.

An interest in sport and organising games for young people led to an offer of part-time employment as an education support worker. This work suited me and although I continued to do seasonal work, I enrolled at university thirteen years after dropping out of high school. During my first year at university, I sat with the Storyteller, the sisters and a group of their peers. He asked me to write down the stories they shared and they all agreed. It was during those university years that I began to develop my appreciation of the value of the teaching I received through Erambie's storytelling tradition. I also started to think about the ways other people view and talk about Indigenous people and culture, with a greater understanding of the importance of sharing positive stories. This book is a celebration of the continuity of Koori storytelling. It retells well-worn stories, many of them entrusted to me by gifted storytellers, and adds new ones I uncovered while walking another track outside of my community.

I came to academic studies with a personal interest and, as it turns out, a measure of knowledge on the subject. As I immersed myself in the ideas other people have about Aborigines in sport, I started making connections between my background knowledge and the sports discourse. I began to question what the sports discourse says about Indigenous people. For years I tried to refine my thoughts well enough to be able to explain my unease with what I read about Indigenous communities beyond saying, 'it just doesn't fit with what I know'.

Overview

I did not set out to write a revisionist account of events that occurred at the elite level of sport. However, by comparing my own experiences with the equally legitimate — but more narrowly focused — stories about race and sport, inevitable differences emerged between knowledge created within my Koori community and knowledge created about us by outsiders. This book questions the foundation of knowledge about Aborigines in sport by offering cultural continuity as an additional framework through which to view the experiences of Aborigines. It tells the reader something more about who we are as a modern Koori community and the role storytelling plays in the continual formation of our identities.

The book is not a detailed history of a particular period of time. The tightest focus is on the period from 1900 to 1960, but there are places where I pick up stories from before and after this period. Non-Indigenous people's descriptions of Koori people consistently emphasised difference and inferiority on the part of Aborigines. I examine the ways that Kooris are described over the entire period of contact from 1815 through to the present day. If I only wanted to record the community's sporting achievements, one clearly defined, historical period would make sense. However, this book is more about how history is constructed so it makes more sense not to restrict myself to a particularly narrow historical period.

This book examines physical activities and sports that are important to Erambie Kooris, including the animated form of storytelling that has a significant physical performance component, games such as rounders and skipping, as well as bare-knuckle fighting. It also examines the connections between physical activities and sports as cultural practices. In doing this, the book gives a picture of daily life, albeit through the lens of sport and physical activity. The reader should get an understanding, not just of the types of racism Aborigines face, but also of our lives independent of mainstream society and the extent to which this life revolves around a distinctively Koori culture. This is important to understand in relation to the concept of authenticity and modern Koori culture. It is also important to consider this alternative reading of a Koori community's experience in sport in relation to the origins of knowledge about our community. The reader should consider not only what is known about Indigenous communities but also where that knowledge comes from.

Some of the chapters include previously published material. Parts of the story were previously melded into a review of literature and published in *Australian Aboriginal Studies*. These previously published parts are put back into place for this book. Chapter One explores the ways that a certain type of discourse developed about Aborigines in sport. These 'straight-line' stories contribute to a broader discourse of deficit where Indigenous communities are represented as inferior. Rather than being a denial of racism, this chapter makes the case that such a discourse runs the risk of creating another, inferior, stereotype of Aborigines. In summarising this discourse, I also consider the importance of theoretical and methodological approaches that are used in creating knowledge in this area. Chapter Two introduces the Koori people who live at Erambie. It gives the reader an idea about who we are and briefly outlines how the Erambie community came to be. This chapter also explains the significance of the Erambie community within Wiradjuri country and gives an account of the rich community life on Erambie, while telling the reader something more than our experiences with racism. I also describe how an extensive repertoire of stories from Erambie's oral history tradition was worked into a manageable and focused set of stories about life on the reserve. In Chapter Three, the floating nature of representation of Aborigines is uncovered through an account of the popular Erambie Allblacks football team that barnstormed the Western District for two decades beginning in 1922. Here, the way non-Indigenous people represented Aborigines during a time of high visibility for these Koori athletes is examined. Although the main focus is on representation, this chapter also considers the significance of a football team to the Erambie community as a further example of cultural continuity.

Chapter Four also deals with contrasting representations in the ways that Indigenous cultural practices can become known. This chapter includes description and an examination of the practice of fighting to settle disputes. The fights at the railway gates are described by those who took part in them, and comparisons are made between their accounts and those of the people who witnessed them as outsiders. Continuing a dual focus on representation and continuity, Chapter Five gives an example of how variations from the common theme of representation can be accommodated. The significance of sport in maintaining community organisation is illustrated in this case study of one 'clever' Wiradjuri family. This chapter also establishes a link between the physically and intellectually outstanding men of pre-contact Wiradjuri culture and those of the Erambie community. Chapter Six draws on my more recent work to build on my own developing understanding of the importance of adding to the predominant ways that Indigenous people are represented in the sports discourse. This chapter offers continuity as an alternative theoretical framework to telling stories about Aborigines. Continuity of culture is one way to understand the many social and cultural differences between mainstream society and the Erambie Wiradjuri community. Chapter Seven highlights the fundamental contrasts in the ways differences are explained. It also makes clear the implications of having an imbalance in the way knowledge in this area is constructed.

Chapter 1

Straight-line stories: Representations and Indigenous Australian identities in sports discourses

Sport, however, has another attribute: it is the avenue by which Aborigines and Islanders have earned and demanded the respect of non-Aboriginal Australia; it has given them a sense of worth and pride, especially since they have had to overcome the twin burdens of racism and opposition on the field. It has shown Aborigines and Islanders that using their bodies is still the one and only way they can compete on equal terms with an often hostile, certainly indifferent, mainstream society. (Tatz & Tatz 2000: 33)

In the aftermath of civil rights victories, the politics of 'victimhood' became the predominant methodology of black advocacy and the reigning paradigm of public policy thinking. (Pearson 2007: 26)

While attending university I found a scholarly discourse about Aborigines that confronted the various forms of racism that made up part of my own experience in sport. This chapter is not a denial of the pervasive nature of racism, nor is it an attack on writers who confront racism. It is about how a particular discourse can become dominant in a discipline. The politics of recognition often leads to a restricted representation of Indigenous Australians and, as discussed here, one in particular that foregrounds deficit and victimhood. Negotiating away from such a discourse is a complex process.

In the politics of representing Indigenous identity it can be risky to allow the discussion to focus on anything other than the ideal of a fair go for all Australians. So, it continues to be politically expedient to use the language of victimhood as Noel Pearson refers to in the quote above. There is a danger here in creating another stereotypically inferior identity by repeatedly considering this one aspect of Indigenous experience when there is a much richer and greater experience to draw from. The literature of Aborigines in sport (with reference to comparable writing from sports journalism) demonstrates the presence of a pervasive discourse of deficit and victimhood. Recognition of this discourse, and developing ways to broaden it, are of critical importance today.

A grievance narrative

Shields, Bishop and Mazawi define deficit thinking as a concept where a group of people are described and explained as deficient. Difference, in deficit thinking, is pathological and linked to power because it relates to what is considered normal (2005). Gorringe, Ross and Fforde have termed the accumulation of deficit representations about Indigenous Australians a 'saturating narrative' (2011: 9). They note the difficulty in moving away from deficit discourse and argue that there is a need to replace negative representations with positive ones. Gorringe, Ross and Fforde reported on an Australian Institute of Aboriginal and Torres Strait Islander Studies workshop that was organised as a 'safe place' for Indigenous people to discuss ways of disengaging from the language of deficit. One participant at the workshop commented, 'it's amazing how quickly you can get white support if you kick black people' (in Gorringe, Ross & Fforde 2011: 11).

Noel Pearson and Marcia Langton are two prominent Indigenous Australians who participate in the discussion of deficit and the politics of identity in Australia. Pearson writes that compelling parallels exist between the experiences of Indigenous Australians and black Americans during the civil rights era (2007). Speaking loudly and often against stereotypes of innate abilities, while detailing examples of racism, were important parts of the efforts to advance the legal rights of black people in America and Australia.

However, in seeking to move on from this discourse, Pearson takes what he calls a 'compelling line' from African-American Booker T Washington to argue that black people should not 'permit our grievances to overshadow our opportunities' (in Pearson 2007: 20). Pearson takes this line as a foundation to his philosophy of participation in mainstream Australian society. He argues that an identity of victimhood (internalising victim status) is 'destructive' and 'demeaning' (2007: 30). Pearson challenges people to consider the consequences of the dominance of the representation of Aborigines as passive victims of racism.[1] Marcia Langton describes the volume of work done by anthropologists to collect humanist data and criticises people who use essentialist representations to grind ideological axes (2011). She points to a hijacking of discourses as a reason to expand the conversation. Pearson and Langton offer a discourse of personhood as an alternative to conversations about victimhood that is yet to be taken up.

Writing about Aborigines in sport is a small academic field, although it is a more common feature in non-academic literature such as biographies and newspapers. However, an overrepresentation of Aborigines in popular sports means that sports fields are significant sites for public representations of Aborigines. Collectively, the academic and non-academic stories told about Aborigines in sport (the dominant discourse) constitute what American columnist and author Jack Cashill has termed a 'grievance narrative':

> We all have grown so used to this shame-on-us school of storytelling that we take it for granted. Today, those who shape our culture — writers, critics, publishers, broadcasters, movie and TV producers — routinely calculate the essence of individuals, especially racial minorities, not as the sum of their blessings but rather as the sum of their grievances. (Cashill 2006: 3)

Prominent in the current politics of identity in Australia, the grievance narrative is of concern because ultimately it restricts representations of Aborigines, as so many other stereotypes have done in the past. Presenting only the image of the Aborigine as victim can constrain how people view Aborigines and how we view ourselves. A look at sports writings over the past five decades illustrates how the dominant discourse on Aborigines in sport uses a language of deficit, which is characteristic of a grievance narrative.

Becoming a researcher

My own experience, going from Erambie into university study, was that the writing about Aborigines in sport told part of the story very well. In 1987, the year Colin Tatz published *Aborigines in sport*, my community's football team was denied entry to a local competition. Subsequent applications in 1996 and 2004 were also denied because, we were told, 'Aboriginal teams are too much trouble'. Having regularly confronted various forms of racism on and off the sports field, I recognised from experience the stories of racism that were common in the literature. However, as I read more of how people were writing about Aborigines in sport, I realised that the whole picture was not represented, and a very significant part of the story was almost completely absent. This absence was emphasised by the discrepancy in how sports stories and stories about community life were told by my own community, and how they were told in the literature.

Within my community, stories about racism were a part of a much broader repertoire held by senior women and men. It was the absence of this broader repertoire in writings about Aborigines that caused me to question how my community was being represented. Reading an accumulating story of deficit in the literature led me to resent the way that Indigenous communities seemed to be unrelentingly represented as terrible places. I felt a responsibility to defend communities such as Erambie from misrepresentation and unfair criticism by outsiders. I concluded that writing about race and sport in Australia was contributing to a dominant discourse that constrained understanding of communities, seeing them as solely negative places. My response was to reject that part of the writing about Aborigines in sport, and instead to seek new ways of writing that could articulate the reality of sports experience, recognise the impact and effect of racism, but do so without engaging and perpetuating a grievance narrative.

Incidences of racism are common enough that the need to confront discrimination, prejudice, racist words and actions is ongoing. However, broadening the discourse will bring the representations of Aborigines in the writing about sport more closely into line with the richer lived experiences of individuals, and this in itself combats racism.

Ideas of representation

This chapter examines what the word 'Aborigine' has come to signify. It focuses on the ways that representations in the discourse about Aborigines in sport accumulate social meanings (Barthes 1957/1972). Cultural theorist Stuart Hall's ideas on production and reception of representations are used here to analyse the ways that common stories are told and heard. Hall's work is an extension of linguistic, anthropological and psychoanalytical theories about difference. Developing theory using the work of Freud, Derrida, Bakhtin, Fanon, Barthes and others, Hall offers four theoretical approaches to explain differences in representation (1997a). The first two are influenced by linguistics, both stating that difference is essential to creating meaning and that meaning can only be constructed in dialogue with an 'other'. The anthropological explanation asserts that meaning is assigned through categorising or ordering. The fourth, psychoanalytical, explanation considers that the 'other' is fundamental to knowledge about the self.

Hall developed his theoretical position to explain representations of race in Britain in the context of social order. One of the key ideas that Hall takes up in developing theory, particularly in relation to the influence of anthropology, is anthropologist Mary Douglas' argument that classification is a universal and rational part of ordered human behaviour (Douglas 1966/2002). Hall summarises how he uses Douglas' work as follows:

> Classification is a very generative thing[,] once you are classified a whole range of other things fall into place as a result of it...It is not just that you have blacks and whites, but of course one group of those people have a much more positive value than the other group. That's how power operates...to ascribe to the black population, characteristics that used to be used for the white ones, generates enormous tension in the society. Mary Douglas...describes this in terms of what she calls 'matter out of place'...You know exactly where you are, you know who are the inferiors and who the superiors are and how each has a rank...What disturbs you is what she calls 'matter out of place'. (Hall 1997b: 2–3)

Martin Nakata, a Torres Strait Islander academic, termed the place where two cultures meet a cultural interface. For Nakata, the cultural interface is a place where all interested people can meet to create knowledge based on a melding of multiple standpoints:

> It is a multi-layered and multi-dimensional space of dynamic relations constituted by the intersections of time, place, distance, different systems of thought, competing and contesting discourses within and between different knowledge traditions. (2007: 10)

Nakata's description of his own encounters with knowledge created about Indigenous Australians, and the Standpoint Theory he developed out of his own efforts to understand them, are also useful in understanding the reception and production of representations (Nakata 2007: 1–12).

What I have taken from Hall and Nakata is that the locations of the writer, and the reader, are critical to reception of representations. Together, Hall's and Nakata's parallel ideas offer a way of explaining the competing narratives I encountered in the ways that stories about Aborigines in sport are told. The typical representations of Aborigines in sport that are included in this book are therefore considered within the wider context in which they were produced.

Ending silence

Much of the academic writing about Aborigines in sport takes the form of historical narrative. The stories that are told span the entire period of colonisation. In this time a lot of unremarkable life has occurred within Indigenous communities and there have been many positive events and developments. However, it is also true that there has been a great inequality of rights, and the discourse on Aborigines in sport has sought in some ways to address this.

DJ Mulvaney's *Cricket Walkabout* was published in the year of the 1967 referendum — and thus as one successful Indigenous rights campaign came to an end. Mulvaney's book joined an emerging discourse about Aborigines and civil rights that challenged racism, in this case by writing about the 1868 cricketers as people and highlighting the restrictions they experienced. Representations of Indigenous Australians mattered during the lead-up to the 1967 referendum (Attwood & Markus 2007; Stokes 1997) and books that challenged the existing place of Aborigines were published during this period (Manne 2003). The year after the referendum, anthropologist WEH Stanner's 'Great Australian Silence' lecture about dispossession and its consequences was broadcast. However, demonstrating the persistence of old-style stereotypes, in the same year Jack Pollard introduced his book, *The Ampol book of Australian sporting records*, with the following statement:

> The Australian aborigine has a fascinating facility for sports which demand whippy reflexes and strong backs. Periodically he has played spectacular roles in Australian sports, ranging from the dramatic delivery of knock-out punches (Ron Richards, Elley Bennett, Jack Hassen, Lionel Rose), to flashing speed on the wings of football teams. He is a superfine fisherman of unorthodox methods (spears, nets, stones), an amazing cross-country runner (up to 200 miles), but often cannot deal with the celebrity sporting success brings. The unpredictable aborigine is an integral part of the Australian sporting scene regardless of whether the game is soccer, amateur or professional fist-fighting, bike riding, sprinting, or cricko. (Pollard 1968: 1)

Pollard reinforced racism by reproducing the stereotyped representations of the physically gifted and unpredictable Aborigine. In doing so, he creates meaning about Aborigines by classifying people according to a preferred order based on an assumed prevailing racial hierarchy that always required Aborigines to be represented as an inferior race.

The field of writing about Aborigines in sport has developed in a social and political context in which representations continue to matter to the ongoing pursuit of civil and human rights. Representations matter because social and political gains are to be found in the democratic process. Although approaching the issue from different perspectives, both Mulvaney and Pollard were writing about difference in the midst of the Freedom Rides of 1965, the Land Rights Acts of the 1960s and 1970s, the creation of the Aboriginal flag as a symbol of unity and difference, and in the lead-up to the establishment of the Tent Embassy in 1972. They were writing at a time when some Indigenous Australians were living in communities that were controlled by government agents. Their books were published just prior to Wiradjuri writer Kevin Gilbert's 1973 classic, *Because a white man'll never do it*, which included the dedication to all Aborigines, whom he referred to as 'patriots' and 'poor buggars all'.

The following decades witnessed a continuing social justice movement and the introduction of landmark legislation. The 1980s saw the Queensland Government declare a state of emergency and make street marches illegal to combat criticism of its Indigenous policy during the 1982 Brisbane Commonwealth Games. There were competing narratives about the Bicentenary in 1988 as either a celebration or an insult. The 1990s witnessed the report on the Royal Commission into Aboriginal Deaths in Custody in 1991, the passage of Native Title legislation in 1993, and in 1994 Cathy Freeman controversially carried the Aboriginal flag on a victory lap at the Commonwealth Games. In the two years following the then Prime Minister Paul Keating's historic 1992 speech in Redfern, high-profile incidents involving club officials, supporters and players in 1993 and 1994 forced the Australian Football League to introduce a Racial and Religious Vilification Rule (Gardiner 1997: Gardiner 2003). So far in this century, in 2005 the elected Indigenous representative body, Aboriginal and Torres Strait Islander Commission, has been abolished; the Racial Discrimination Act was suspended to allow the federal government's 'Intervention' in some Indigenous communities; and a National Apology was offered in 2007 for racist acts by past governments.

Strategic representations

Amidst the historical context briefly outlined above, the language of deficit was established early on in the writing about Aborigines in sport. In reference to the idea of an egalitarian society — which, as Kane notes, is so central to Australian national identity (1997) — it was necessary to point out the difference in how Aborigines and non-Aborigines were treated. Repeatedly demonstrating unfairness was the dominant method used to challenge racism, and by doing so the use of this type of discourse challenged the ideal of an egalitarian society.

In his 1980 article, 'Professional Aboriginal boxers in Eastern Australia 1930–1979', Richard Broome asserts that there is a 'basic oppression' of Aborigines (69). Similarly, in his 1984 biography of the rugby-playing Ella brothers, Bret Harris introduces the La Perouse community (where the Ella family lived) in the following manner:

> La Perouse is Sydney's Soweto, the inverse mirror image of the Lucky Country. It is difficult to imagine the Aboriginal ghetto, on the inhospitable peninsula which juts into Botany Bay south of the city, is only a 10 minute drive from some of the most expensive and exclusive real estate in Australia. (1984: 9)

Although Harris does quote May Ella's more positive memories of one aspect of life at La Perouse — 'Rodney [the oldest of the Ella boys] was spoiled with affection. His sisters doted on him and his uncles could hardly wait to teach him how to play football' — his writing focuses on the negative aspects of their environment (1984: 13). In focussing so strongly on a negative description of 'Sydney's Soweto' in the 'Lucky Country' and using words such as 'ghetto' and 'inhospitable' to demonstrate stark differences between Aboriginal and non-Aboriginal Australia, he confirmed Hall's theory that meaning is created through representations of opposites (Harris 1984: 13). Harris also references Australian national identity against the more readily acknowledged racism of South Africa as he challenged Australians to compare his representation of Aborigines to what they knew about Apartheid. The similarities in background between the Ella brothers and that of many white Australian athletes, and the positives in the story May Ella told about her son developing sporting talent, are brief. Harris concluded his introduction with the summary statement:

> Society has a duty to foster Aboriginal sporting talent. In the past sport has been possibly the only area in which Aborigines have been able to achieve any sort of equality with Europeans. This is largely because of the Aborigines' physical prowess. But it is also a reflection of the limited avenues open to Aborigines to express themselves. (1984: 21)

The representations of Aborigines in the developing field of sport writing were by necessity not neutral. They were written to confront racism. Colin Tatz brought an approach to the discourse that was political, economic and legal. Where Mulvaney, Broome and Harris had written in detail about specific sports, Tatz wrote in more general terms about racism through the lens of sport. Tatz's approach was to build an overall picture using less detailed evidence from a number of sports. In *Aborigines in sport* (1987) he set out his argument that sport mirrors a general racism in Australian society. He also cited Pollard, Mulvaney, Broome, and Harris in making his case that Aborigines are victims of racism and non-Indigenous Australians are the victimisers. Tatz's work since *Aborigines in sport* has generally repeated this theme, both in format and content. Even though it contains more research and analysis, his landmark text *Obstacle race: Aborigines in sport* (1995a), essentially advances the same arguments. The essence of what Tatz has written on the subject is captured in the following passage:

> Sport is a mirror of many things. It reflects political, social, economic and legal systems. It also reflects the Aboriginal experience, especially since 1850. While playing fields are not places where people expect to find, or want to see, racial discrimination, sport is an important indicator of Australian racism...Denial of competition takes three forms. One is structural: because of their place in the political, legal, economic and social system, Aborigines and Islanders rarely go onto squash courts or Group 1 golf courses or into ski lodges. They never hang glide, play polo, ride bikes for Yamaha or drive cars for Ferrari. The second form is institutional: on settlements and missions — where many Aborigines have lived — there was, literally, no grass. There were no facilities such as coaches and physiotherapists, and scholarships are not part of their vocabulary or experience even in today's 'communities' which were, so recently, settlements and missions. Finally, there is blatant racism: the exclusion of individuals or teams from competition because they are Aboriginal. (Tatz & Tatz 2000: 7)

Accounts such as this tell a story about Aborigines in sport that parallels those told about African-American sportspeople in the United States. The dominant stories of discrimination against Aborigines and African-Americans in sport emerged out of similar struggles for recognition and power. Harry Edwards, an African-American sociologist and one-time activist who advocated boycotts at the Mexico Olympics to draw attention to issues of race, is prominent among those in the US who argue that black over-representation in sport can be traced back to an oppressive environment. Thus, for example, Edwards writes: 'black athletic superiority results from a "complex of societal conditions" that channels a disproportionate number of talented blacks into athletic careers' (in Hoberman 1997: 195). The dominant discourse in writing about Aborigines in sport is aligned with Edwards' social mobility paradigm. Thus, as early as 1984, Colin Tatz made his position clear: '...the answers lie in the social structure of both society and of sport...I share Edwards' rejection of the biological determinism mythology. My view is that blacks excel where and when they are hungry and needy' (1984: 13).

Tatz's argument is linked intrinsically to race due to his belief that Aborigines succeed solely because of an impetus provided by the colonial racial experience, as opposed to any of the other reasons why an individual, regardless of ethnic background, might achieve in this realm. In doing so, writing on this subject, although framed to combat racism, continues in effect to engage with the racial paradigm of earlier writings that established an essential connection between Aboriginal sporting achievement and racism. This approach is consistent with historical writing that some have strategically labelled a politically correct attack on national identity, known as a 'black armband' view (McKenna 1997).

Accumulating power in the meaning of 'difference'

During most of the 1990s, little new primary material was added to the field. In this period there was a compelling restating by a number of authors of the general theme that sport mirrors racism in Australian society. For example, Tatz mostly repackaged his original argument from *Aborigines in sport* (1995a; Tatz & Tatz 1996), and the work of Cashman (1995) and Adair and Vamplew (1997) contributed two more overviews of the field but added little new information.[2]

Hall argues that representations gain meaning by being read in connection with one another, and that these accumulate meaning together (1997a: 4). In the 1990s, the writing in the field of Aborigines in sport accumulated meaning through repetition of the story of inequality. In citing each other (for example, Cashman repeatedly references Tatz, and Adair and Vamplew reference Tatz and Cashman) the authors accumulated meaning together. While they built a strong case against racism, these texts are also limited in the way they represent Aborigines. Their writings are full of references to deficit, even when telling stories of success. Thus, Harris writes about 'poverty' (1989: 7); Tatz about 'the hungriest of people' (1995a: 11), a lack of 'self worth', 'pride' and 'respect' (Tatz 1995b: 54), and refers to Indigenous 'communities' in inverted commas (Tatz & Tatz 1996: 1). Cashman discusses 'improved social and economic status', 'social acceptance' and 'upward mobility' (1995: 146), while Adair and Vamplew write about a contrast between Aborigines who unsuccessfully struggle to maintain tribal culture and 'well-to-do Australians' (1997: 67).

Focusing on difference continues to be strategically necessary in the politics of identity in the first decade of the twenty-first century, and this creates meaning about Aborigines. Writing about Aborigines continues to address racism because racism continues to be part of society and sport. Both the fight against racism and the connected use of deficit language in sports writing are ongoing today. Examples are commonplace. Academic Stella Coram argues that Indigenous athletes 'by virtue of their history are political' and that Indigenous athletes come from 'impoverished communities' that are 'used to abject oppression' (2001: 92). She tells a story of 'rags to riches' about successful Indigenous athletes (2001: 97). Greg Gardiner tells a similar story of Aborigines who have to overcome racism to succeed (2003). Sport, writes Gardiner, 'has provided Indigenous people with one of the few avenues for participation and success in mainstream culture' (2003: 31). Sean Gorman argues for sport as a place for understanding and changing society and that it is a place for 'struggle and resistance' (2008: 189). He updates and contextualises racist incidents similar to the ones uncovered by Tatz and others in the 1980s. Nowhere has the case for sport being an ally to Indigenous Australians been made more vividly than in Gorman's description of AFL legend Nicky Winmar's first day as a roustabout in a West Australian shearing shed (2011). On the back cover of Lauren Calloway's story of the life of Indigenous jockey Darby McCarthy, the reader is asked to consider how 'this half blood black fella from a squalid camp in Cunnamulla became one of the really significant Indigenous Australians of the 20th century' (2004). The book details

McCarthy's life through a lens of both institutional and individual racism and tells us how he defied 'the expectations of a small country town entrenched in racism' (Calloway 2004: xiv).

It is not untrue to write that sport is one avenue to success for Aborigines. However, following only this approach constrains understanding of Indigenous engagement in sport in its variety and complexity. Individual identity (personhood) takes a back seat when an athlete such as McCarthy becomes an Aborigine, jockey and victim of racism (victimhood) instead of Darby McCarthy the jockey. Framing identities in this way contributes to the grievance narrative outlined above and the development and persistence of stereotypes — and this in itself contributes to the perpetuation of racism.

Richard Broome's writing on Aborigines in sport shows how difficult it can be to move away from the dominant discourse. With a greater understanding of agency and power, in 1996 Broome revised his 1980 story about Indigenous boxers. He added that Aborigines were 'not only being victims' but also 'agents and manipulators of that power and discourse' (1996: 2). Broome described his change in position in the following way:

> Through teaching, researching and reading Aboriginal history since 1980, reading the works of English Historian E.P. Thompson, and also listening to my colleagues in women's history, I have developed a stronger sense of power from below and the agency held by Aboriginal historical actors. (1996: 1)

Ultimately, Broome returns to the dominant discourse by adding that such agency 'might be transitory and subsequently overlaid by experiences of injustice and discrimination in reserves, country towns and other situations' (1996: 2). In addition, he later argues that sport 'made them [Aboriginal sportspeople] feel the equal of other Victorians' (2005: 225).

The dominant discourse has been summarised in at least one international journal as representative of the story of Indigenous Australians:

> Tatz...concludes that "Aboriginal sporting success, no matter how brief or tragic, has given Aborigines more uplift, more collective pride, more Kudos than any other single activity"...[Broome] on the same subject...assert[s] that gains are short term, diversionary, and, ultimately, destructive[,] reinforcing the Aboriginals' 'basic oppression'. (Sammons 1994: 248)

Although in 2009 Tatz and Adair recently restated the argument that racism in varying degrees is the 'essence of Aboriginal and Islander sport' (5), their guest-edited edition of *Australian Aboriginal Studies* is notable as it also includes some new perspectives. For example, in her paper 'Sport, physical activity and urban Indigenous young people', Alison Nelson interviewed a number of young Indigenous people and her findings challenged 'some of the commonly held assumptions and "knowledges" about Indigenous young people and their engagement in physical activity…[including]…their "natural" ability, and the use of sport as a panacea for health, education and behavioural issues' (Nelson 2009: 101). She found in her interviews that there was very little discussion about sport as resistance to racism and that:

> [m]ultiple, shifting and complex identities were expressed in the young people's articulation of the place and meaning of sport and physical activity in their lives. They both engaged in, and resisted, dominant Western discourses regarding representations of Indigenous people in sport. The paper gives voice to these young people in an attempt to disrupt and subvert hegemonic discourses. (2009: 101)

Nelson also noted the importance of representation to the production of knowledge. She argues against 'pathologising' Aborigines and suggests privileging Indigenous voices can lead to consideration of 'strengths and diversity' (103). Nelson contrasts the representations of identity she found among young Aborigines with the 'constant representations being made over time' that feed ideas of deficit and disempower Aborigines (102). Nelson's paper demonstrates that restrictive representations can be challenged by empowering Indigenous voices. However, it is important also to note that privileging Indigenous voices can reinforce *or* challenge a dominant discourse.

Talking back:
Indigenous voices at the interface

Indigenous voices have been heard on the topic of sport in varying degrees. Privileging Indigenous voices changes the discourse by blending in more complex representations of identity. Lynette Russell describes how a number of Indigenous identities can be blended into a representation (2001). The phrase 'blending of identities' is also a good way to describe what privileging Indigenous voices adds to the discourse.

Bernard Whimpress accepts discrimination as one aspect of the sporting experience for Aboriginal people, but his account is not dominated by this theme (1999). His work is thus important in the current analysis because it provides a wider perspective, unconstrained by a dominant deficit discourse. For example, when discussing the introduction of cricket during the mission era, Whimpress makes the following observations about the ways that Aborigines played western sports:

> It would be far-fetched to claim that cricket played by Aborigines in the nineteenth century was *corroborised* although in matches such as those at Point McLeay, Corranderrk and Poonindie there are elements of play and resistance, of turning cricket on its head…In traditional society the way the boomerang was thrown was important. Similarly, the way that runs were scored could be more important than the number of them. (1999: 43)

Writing about Indigenous cricketer Faith Thomas, Whimpress identifies a variation of experience not previously found in writing about Aborigines in sport (2002). Thomas indicated to Whimpress that she had little experience of racism in sport when growing up in a small country town.

John Perry also makes some changes to the established style of discourse. Perry recognises that to get 'even a partial and extremely limited insight into what happened' to Indigenous champion sprinter Bobby Kinnear, a researcher must 'travel to his home ground and have a look at where he started his run' (2002: 186). In doing this himself, Perry found — in much the way as Whimpress found with Faith Thomas — that Koori informants told stories that 'did not harp on the theme of pathos so central to white depictions of their people' (2002: 186). Still, Perry does summarise Kinnear's victory as a symbol of resistance to oppression:

> His great run came to symbolise for Aboriginal people the refusal of their forebears to sit down and expire under the burden of oppression. From this perspective sporting achievements can be looked on as acts of resistance. (2002: 193)

The contributions that blend representations of resistance with other Indigenous identities are different in their tone to those that focus more narrowly on deficit. Aboriginality as tradition (persistence) is one common representation added to the established identity of Aboriginality as resistance.

Indigenous voices and prolonged observations underpin Brian McCoy's writing about football within an Indigenous community. In many places McCoy writes from personal observations but it is clear that his in-depth understanding of witnessed events is supplemented by the voices of people in the community he writes about. He writes extensively about differences in a way that does not suggest deficit (2002). In fact, the romanticised tone of McCoy's description can be read as an argument that Kimberley desert communities play football in ways that are superior to non-Indigenous players:

> There are also other relationships at work on the football field. Most are hidden to the non-Indigenous world for these relationships are born and nurtured in men's Law ceremonies. These relationships reflect an even deeper bond between men and they demand even further respect, even avoidance, for some men from others. Visitors to communities will not know of these relationships and might wonder as a player appears to hang back from tackling another too aggressively. Strong men's business can exist even here on the football field. (2002: 32)

In a chapter on football, McCoy weaves football into a discussion about life for Indigenous men. Alongside a discussion of history, health and prison, among other topics, he again writes that 'football offers young men the continuity of being held by older men that began and was promised in Law' (2008: 145), and adds a description of football played in accordance with cultural values:

> If the deceased was a footballer...the playing area needed to be 'opened up' before competition could begin. This could be achieved by a group of women moving in single file around the oval, crying and sweeping the ground with leafy branches...removing signs of where the deceased has been and walked. (2008: 150)

The biography of members of the McAdam family, as told to Elizabeth Tregenza, is an example of a complex and nuanced story (McAdam 1995). Where others tell stories about what happens to Aborigines at the elite level of sport, Tregenza wanders through the lives of the people who went on to become elite football players. When the subject of race and sport is considered, the reader can put those stories into context because they know more about the players as people than the racism they have faced.

Even though race and racism are parts of the story that Tregenza tells, it is difficult to essentialise the McAdam family given the variety of topics covered. Tregenza allows family members to tell for themselves how generations of their experiences led to excellence in sport. Significantly, the family's humour, shared human values and connections to culture are covered in some detail. Tregenza, the narrator, stands aside to let Indigenous storytellers speak. What results is a complex explanation of excellence in sport. Charlie McAdam, father of Australian Football League players Gilbert, Greg and Adrian, tells the reader, 'the stories of my people go back to the time the sea covered the land and the moon was a young man fishing in the Ponton River' (McAdam 1995: 4). Of station life he says, 'I remember I used to have really good times at the station with all my playmates, my cousins and the others' (7). McAdam and his sons tell stories about their lives and how they came to excel at sport. They cover topics such as hunting, initiation and teaching alongside discussion of shared human values and experiences of country life. When race and racism are discussed, the inclusion of stories about family, culture and joy give a more rounded picture of the McAdams as people who live complex lives that are not necessarily dominated by poverty, oppression and racism; their experience is not portrayed as one that is solely in opposition to (and thus controlled by) the dominant culture. Writing about Aborigines in sport is gradually expanding the conversation, mostly due to an increase of Indigenous voices.

Writing back

Further expansion in the field to include Indigenous voices as writers creates a more dynamic space from where the complexities of Indigenous experiences in sport (and society) continue to emerge. Some Indigenous writers have been critical of the representations of Aborigines in sport. Their response appears to be similar to Nakata's description of his response to reading representations of his own people which contributed to his development of Standpoint Theory (2007).

Worimi historian John Maynard wrote hopefully in predicting that Aborigines would find a place in the writing of Australian history (2002). With its goal of telling an untold story of participation in one sport, Maynard's *Aboriginal stars of the turf: Jockeys of Australian racing history* tells a history that is characterised by more than racism (2002). Maynard's later work again uncovered Indigenous histories in *The Aboriginal soccer tribe* (2011). Like Whimpress (1999), Maynard believes that Indigenous stories had been 'derided, hidden and even erased' but persevered to 'lift and reveal rich tales of survival and inspiration' (2002: v).

Daryle Rigney labelled the lack of Indigenous voices in the sports literature oppressive. He argues the need for 'revisiting and rewriting the events, processes and history from an Indigenous perspective' in order to develop writing in the field that he criticises as historically 'limited in its quality' (2003: 48). Barry Judd and Chris Hallinan make similar judgements about 'the discourse on Aboriginality' that is 'characterised by essentialist understandings of identity':

> The construction of Aboriginal identity in the literature of Australian sport and sporting history continues to reply [sic] on simplistic notions of indigeneity which do little more than reiterate the colonial myths, fears and desires of the past. (Judd & Hallinan 2008:19)

Judd writes that identity is 'central to any consideration of Aborigines in sport' (2005: 32).

Larissa Behrendt has called for the Australian media to accept 'all the parts that make us human...not just the easy parts that do not raise awkward questions about the continuing inequality between Indigenous people and all other Australians' (2001: 29). The increase in Indigenous voices does not result in less awkward questions being asked. It does increase the variety of viewpoints of the story told and makes us more human. The parts that Indigenous voices add to the story include Indigenous viewpoints on existing topics related to race, representation, power, inequality and identity. In addition, continuity of culture is a frequent theme in Indigenous writing on sport.

Heidi Norman's history of the annual NSW rugby league Knockout shows how a contemporary sport has also been used by Kooris as a vehicle for a number of important values and meanings:

Every aspect of this event speaks to Indigenous realities. In documenting this event perhaps a new account of Aboriginal history might be discerned in the context of self-determination, or at least a period 'more free' of the oppressive role of the Aboriginal [sic] Welfare Board. The field of Aboriginal history necessarily hovers around black and white relations, while the focus of this all-Aboriginal celebratory event is only briefly concerned with non-Aboriginal relations. But this is not to falsely elevate Indigeneity as a rarefied, separate reality, but rather to understand how this event emerged from particular experiences that are both culturally continuous in a traditional sense and historically produced. (2006: 170)

Using interviews from people who participated in the event, Norman describes continuity of culture in a contemporary sports event alongside a discussion of political, economic and racial issues. She describes how the Knockout is used to maintain and even re-establish kinship and relationships to country. In 2009 Norman writes about the Knockout as a political event. However, representations of difference can be both positive and negative and they can be read as having multiple meanings (Hall 1997a). When read in comparison to McCoy's description of football in north-western Australia, Norman's description of the Knockout can also be read as an attempt at authentication of identity for Aborigines from the south-east of Australia. Norman approaches difference in a number of ways. She writes the familiar story of inequality in treatment while adding a story of cultural difference as it relates to authenticity of identity. However, the blending of narratives of persistence with the narrative of resistance (Russell 2001) could also be read as an essentialist representation of a homogenous Indigenous identity. It could create an essentialised identity based on the 'cultural Aborigine' (Langton 2011: 13).

In a *Sydney Morning Herald* article entitled 'A Knockout blow to racial stereotypes' (2 October 2010) Debra Jopson draws upon quotes that refer to the Knockout as both a cultural event and a form of resistance:

Football is a byproduct of this weekend. The major focus of most people who come is to catch up because we are in the majority. No matter what happens, 'Aboriginality is in the ascendancy', says Bob Morgan,

61, one of the knockout's founders and original players...For many indigenous people the knockout is the year's social highlight, 'bigger than Christmas', or looking further back, the cultural successor to four-day corroborees, says Aboriginal historian, Heidi Norman...'It is like the lifeblood in their communities...Taking the trophy is the greatest moment of their lives,' says another of the founders, Bob Smith...Says Morgan: 'We spend most of our time struggling for our rights and freedoms. This is the opportunity to celebrate.' (Jobson 2010)

Two narratives from another Indigenous researcher, Darren Godwell, reinforce the idea that representations from Indigenous people are context-dependant, just like those from non-Indigenous authors. Godwell collected testimony from eight Indigenous rugby league Knockout players for his unpublished 1997 Masters thesis to examine the meaning that his informants attributed to their experiences. A substantial amount of testimony emerged that indicated that the men played football for more than just reasons related to resisting racism. One interviewee in Godwell's study suggested that community prestige was a factor in participation in Allblacks carnivals (1997: 57). Another responded that community identity was important and that participation in these carnivals 'goes with the whole image of your community. It's the biggest event on the Aboriginal calendar. People love to hang out for that three day week-end. They get together and see their people, and it brings the community together' (in Godwell 1997: 57).

In his analysis, Godwell hints at the idea of continuity when he suggests that the football carnivals have internal value as ways to maintain connections to tribal identity:

> These carnivals also offer the chance for Aboriginal people to personalise their culture and their traditions. In everyday life Aborigines are contrasted against the non-Aboriginal world which encompasses their lives. In these all-Aboriginal spaces differentiation is made not by skin colour but by tribal, geographic lineage and Aboriginal heritage. This process very much personalises being Aboriginal by redefining the importance of elders, geographic boundaries, cultural differences, languages and tribal affiliations. In this sense the carnivals provide a rare contemporary chance to reaffirm such connections...At a more

symbolic level what activity better represents community identity than having two brightly uniformed teams competing against each other in a decisive competition — a knockout where only the winners move to the next round? At all levels these carnivals offer something for Aboriginal people. (1997: 60–1)

One important part of this analysis is that Godwell considers sport as a space where Indigenous, Australian and human values are maintained. Discussion of connections to place, people and the symbolism of Aboriginal-only sporting competition are impressively woven through the analysis. Support for this point of view is found in the testimony of Indigenous people and it is clear that the theoretical discussion Godwell conducts has come from the words and ideas of the people being studied. In this analysis, Godwell writes that sport has value to Indigenous people in part, but not only, because it fits in with existing values and cultural practices.

Godwell used the testimony from his Masters thesis to focus much more narrowly on racism when he published material from the thesis (2000). For example, while positive quotes about continuity such as the one above are not published, he does use quotes about negative experiences with racism:

Yeah, a bad experience. They had a negative experience — yeah and those bad experiences that they may have, they last forever, you know — you know, whether they got ripped off in the grand final, or whatever. And it comes back to — 'these bastards are doing it again! And they're doing it to *us* again!' (in Godwell 2000: 18)

Godwell's later work is similar to that of Broome (1996) in that it demonstrates how difficult it can be to move away from a discourse of deficit (2000). Godwell reduced the variety of experiences of the men he had interviewed for his thesis to make two main political points. The first point is that their sporting experiences were related to their Indigenous identity as colonised people. The second was that racism restricted opportunities in rugby league. Although these experiences are significant, as Godwell had shown in his earlier Masters thesis, they are not the sole story of Aborigines in sport.

By joining the discourse about race and sport, Indigenous Australians have added rich detail to existing stories while inviting outsiders to share experiences not previously heard about. The result is an expanding discourse that tells more about Aborigines as people (individually and collectively) than only the sum of our grievances.

Representations about Aborigines articulated by Indigenous people rely on difference to create meaning in the same way that non-Indigenous writers do. This means that they can use the same methods and theoretical frameworks of understanding and produce similar types of stories. The field becomes more dynamic, though, as Indigenous people respond to restrictive representations, add insights from insider perspectives, challenge the dominance of certain narratives and reverse positions of dominance in the binary of difference. Even the addition of essentialist representations from Indigenous voices makes for a more complex picture.

Straight-line stories

The same remains the same, riveted onto itself. (Foucault 1966/ 2002: 28)

Us blackfellas don't tell stories in a straight line, we go all the way around it. (Gamilaroi teacher, Laurie Crawford, pers. com.)

Representations of Indigenous Australians are not neutral. Writing about Aborigines in sport is dominated by a discourse of deficit. However, such discourse is not alone in being read from a number of ideological positions. Sticking to stories about grievances is politically expedient: any concession of Indigenous advantage could be co-opted by people with ideological axes to grind. Therefore, saturating the discourse with deficit language may be necessary to confront racism, create change and respond to politicised readings, but it has also created an essentialised and constraining image of Aborigines. Differences are represented as a binary where Aborigines are the victims and non-Aborigines the victimisers.

Mary Douglas' ideas about all matter having a place in an ordered society highlights the danger of drawing from one aspect of rich and varied experience to accumulate language of deficit. One reading of the dominant discourse tells us that Australian society does not live up to the ideal of the fair go. Another way to read the same language of deficit is that Indigenous communities are inferior to the rest of the country. The differences that are described in the discourse contribute to reinforcing this order. The same remains the same because Indigenous Australian communities are pathologised as deficient. The locating of Indigenous communities as inferior is not at issue in political debate. I read in the discourse two versions of one story about deficit.

In the early 1980s, I was a young boy playing football with my mates at Erambie. We ran, kicked, jumped and tackled around and over a sewerage blockage that caused human waste to run through an open ditch along the side of the dirt streets. Josie, a senior Erambie woman born in 1938, was among the women who spoke loudly and often about the injustice of living under such conditions when white people in the town did not. The women told a straight-line story to people from outside the community in order to create change where it was needed. In this respect she essentialised our community identity as victims of racism just as writers about Aborigines in sport were doing.

When outsiders were not around, Josie and other respected senior men and women within the community talked about racism as just one of a greater repertoire of stories. They focused much more on telling about the wonderful life they experienced within the mission community. They spoke carefully about the achievements of elders, great sporting events within the community (and some shared with outsiders). They talked about the essence of our culture being sharing and caring for each other and the importance of maintaining our own ways of being. They talked about what made our community a great place to live. The dominant discourse within the community was not about deficit. It was focused on the advantages of being part of the Erambie community.

In the quote above, Crawford refers to stories told in certain contexts when he says that stories are not told in a straight line. Aborigines do sometimes tell straight-line stories because, as Langton observes, essentialist representations of difference are the foundation of Indigenous activism in modern Australia (2011). There are a few stories being added to the discourse that do not represent difference as deficit. However, there is work left to do so that a complex, nuanced representation of Aborigines as more than the sum of our grievances can be told, without vindicating critics who seek to impose an alternative reading of Aborigines as irresponsible. The challenge, the responsibility, of those who write and read in this area is to locate middle ground where we can offer more stories that share human experiences in sport without the constraints imposed by a deficit discourse.

Chapter 2

Telling stories: People and places

> I was on Erambie mission in Cowra in the early 1980s, sitting on a chair on the lawn while one of the guys cut my hair. An older Wiradjuri man saw us and came up to tell me to make sure I picked up every bit of hair when we finished. No explanation, just 'You don't want to leave that lying around now'. He moved on, and as he did, a young woman sitting with others on the grass turned to me with a nod, 'Yeah, you could get sung, you know!' She smiled but it was clear she was serious and sharing his concern. While I personally do not know of Wiradjuri people who train these days in the arts of sorcery, it is nevertheless an ever-present fact of life…I was surprised by this man's comment. Not by his obvious reference to the existence of spiritual powers or forces which can be mobilised by people, but because this man had, earlier that very day, been at pains to convince me that my studies of 'culture' in Wiradjuri country were misconceived — there was no culture left…[H]e was…devaluing the culture that he and others around him were actually living.
> (Macdonald 2001: 176)

My understanding of what it means to be a Wiradjuri person has been greatly influenced by my interaction with the storytelling tradition of the

Erambie community. Senior men and women who take on the responsibility of being community historians impact upon my own Wiradjuri identity. In many ways, they teach young people in our community how to be Wiradjuri. The continued presence of people from earlier historical periods in stories represents a form of continuity across generations. This continuity is central to Wiradjuri identity.

The Wiradjuri

Wiradjuri historians Mary Coe and Iris Clayton write about a nation of people of 'the three rivers' in central New South Wales; Coe adds that the Wiradjuri clans occupied 'their lands' around the Wambool, Kalare and Murrumbidjeri — Macquarie, Lachlan and Murrumbidgee rivers — since time began (Coe 1989: viii; Clayton & Barlow 1997: 27). The Wiradjuri nation, bordered by high mountain ranges in the east, spreads across rich valleys in an area of New South Wales roughly twice the size of the United Kingdom (Coe 1989; Clayton & Barlow 1997). Estimates of the number of people speaking a common language range from Coe's 12,000 to Clayton and Barlow's 100,000, which made Wiradjuri one of the largest of the Aboriginal nations (Coe 1989; Clayton & Barlow 1997).

Wiradjuri identities as a colonised 'other' are constantly evolving. By 1839 the Narrundjera clan of the Wiradjuri had declared war on the whites and had 'brought in allies' including warriors from the Lachlan River area (Gammage 1986: 32). After repeated victories by the Wiradjuri in these fights, the Commissioner for Crown Lands for the district said, 'the blacks have gone so far and struck such terror into the minds of settlers, that the white inhabitants will be compelled to abandon at least fifty miles of the river' (in Gammage 1986: 34). Gammage writes of this period that the 'Narrundjera and their allies' had cleared white people from well over 100 km of river and even further east whites lived in great dread and went about in well armed parties' (1986: 34). An early white settler observed, 'the tribe had made themselves much dreaded' (in Gammage 1986: 36). This suggests that the Lachlan River clans were at once dreaded among white settlers in the south and 'tolerated' in their home territory where the conflicts had largely subsided (Craze & Marriott 1988: 5).

By the 1840s white people were established on the Lachlan and Murrumbidgee rivers. It was during this period that the Wiradjuri had significant contact with government officials when Crown Lands Commissioners were given the role of Protector of Aborigines (Gammage 1986: 36). The Protectors' personal opinions appear to have greatly influenced the way they described the Wiradjuri in their reports. For example, two Commissioners in the 1840s gave varying representations of the Wiradjuri. In March 1842 Commissioner Beckham wrote that 'the natives could never be improved for they filled their lives with wandering, dancing with their friends from the Lachlan' (in Gammage 1986: 36). He added that, despite the kindness of settlers, 'the Wiradjuri were bound to die out'. Beckham repeated his message yearly that 'the settlers were kind but the blacks intractable — they were doomed' (in Gammage 1986: 36). In contrast, the next government official to report on the characteristics of the Wiradjuri, Henry Bingham, appears to have been more appreciative of them as people. His children had been saved from drowning by the Wiradjuri and Bingham wrote about the 'noble, kind and praiseworthy conduct' of the Wiradjuri (in Gammage 1986: 36). Bingham also noted the objections of Wiradjuri elders to their kinsmen associating too much with white people for fear of a 'threat to ancient customs' (in Gammage 1986: 36–7).

The people making up the Wiradjuri nation at the time of dispossession are the ancestors of the people living in Wiradjuri country today. Descendants of the Murrumbidgee and Lachlan River clans considered bound to die out, along with neighbouring Ngunnawal clans, are living at Erambie.

Connections

Cowra sits on a bend in the Lachlan River, just over 300 kilometres from Sydney. The landscape is dominated by a rocky hill on the eastern side of the river known locally as Billy Goat Hill; the town nestles around it. A small group of Wiradjuri lived in one camp on the western side of the river two kilometres from the town when, in 1890, a thirty-two acre parcel of land was gazetted as an Aboriginal reserve; it became known as Mulyan. The Wiradjuri had decided to settle. An Aborigines Protection Board manager was appointed to supervise the reserve in 1924 and Erambie became a Board-managed station.[1]

The school at the reserve was renamed because it had the same name as the Mulyan school at Wellington. Erambie, the Wiradjuri word for waterhole, was chosen as a replacement. Over time the community also became known as Erambie. Despite its unremarkable beginning, Erambie distinguished itself as an important site where the Wiradjuri confronted the inequalities of life in the mission era. Most importantly, it was a place where kinship ties were retained — and continues to be so.

One noteworthy musician embodies the traditional movement pattern that Wiradjuri people used to continue old kinship ties in spite of interference. Alfred 'Knocker' Williams was born in 1896 into a prominent Wiradjuri family at Brungle near the Tumut River, where the Brungle Station was established in 1888, 152 kilometres south of Erambie (Read 1988). Williams' mother followed traditional movement patterns her entire life and her children were born at various Wiradjuri communities (Read 1988). Knocker was raised mostly at Warangesda Mission, the Christian 'Camp of Mercy' established near the Murrumbidgee in 1880 (Clayton & Barlow 1997: 14).

In 1915 Knocker was living at Edgerton, a Ngunnawal station on the fringes of Yass, less than 100 kilometres north-east of Brungle. At Yass, local government officials acted to move the Ngunnawal from the vicinity of the town (Clayton & Barlow 1997: 57). Fed up with conflict, a number of Ngunnawal families moved from Yass to live at Erambie. Knocker also moved to Erambie after a brief return to Warangesda, from where he was expelled along with two cousins in 1916 (Read 1984a). He then joined his brother at Erambie where he had a son with a Ngunnawal woman before marrying into the prominent Murray family. A reduction in the number of reserves and stations in Wiradjuri country reaffirmed the axis of Warangesda, Brungle, Yass and Erambie (Read 1984a). While Knocker was living at Erambie, in 1924, Warangesda was closed (Clayton & Barlow 1997). Prior to 1924, Erambie must have been an attractive option for the Wiradjuri because of the family connections and unmanaged status of the reserve. It was one of the few unmanaged places to which they could move. From the implementation of the 1909 Act to 1920 the number of people living on or near Erambie grew to more than 150 (Read 1984b; Rimas-Kabaila 1996). This led to complaints from white people in Cowra. However, the 1920s marked the end of a cycle of establishing and destroying reserves. The Aborigines Protection Board realised that it could not continually destroy reserves and placate white people who complained when Aborigines moved too close to towns. This realisation contributed to Erambie's survival (Read 1984b). Erambie actually thrived and, by the 1930s, it was too large to destroy (Read 1984b; Rimas-Kabaila 1996). Knocker was a valued elder at Erambie for many years. However, he returned to live near the Murrumbidgee where he helped establish a Wiradjuri community on the outskirts of Narrandera (Read 1984a). He was joined at Narrandera by Wiradjuri/Ngunnawal families from Erambie (Rimas-Kabaila 1996).

Back at Erambie, old ways flourished unnoticed by outsiders even as residents were asserting independence in response to government intrusions in their lives (Read 1988). By the 1940s the 'special character' of Erambie was beginning to be apparent to the Board. Reports about the problem station — which was regarded as one of the most difficult in the state to manage — followed, and residents were termed 'trouble makers', 'irresponsible' and 'backward' by the Board (Read 1984a: 7–8). The special character of the Erambie community was that the residents demanded their rights and asserted equality with white people (Read 1988). In 1949 an inspector claimed that gaining membership of the local Labor League had 'gone to their heads', they were 'cheeky in their new found knowledge' and that they 'showed little respect for the Board's kindness' (Read 1988: 92). As a cost for their demands for equality and self-management, the residents of Erambie lived with the real threat of children being removed. Still, Erambie's leaders continued to demand equality and assert interminable ownership of the land.

The mission residents took exception to the rules enforced by the managers. For example, working men were expected to seek permission from the managers before inviting friends to their homes and restrictions were even placed on who could attend children's birthday parties (Read 1988). Respected Erambie elders considered such entry rules degrading. They believed they should be 'above that sort of thing' (Read 1988: 95).

Refusal to submit to such restrictions is a recurring theme in the accounts of life on the managed reserve. 'The older people of the past are still lovingly and appreciatively remembered for the stands they took against harsh managers or general injustices' (Macdonald 1986: 99). It was in the indignant atmosphere of the houses of Erambie that the elders gave their 'gift' of 'radicalism' to their children (Read 1984b: 10). The radical, politically active community at Erambie is a place where Wiradjuri culture is continued. Kin-based relationships were and are maintained, and a storytelling tradition still thrives.

The special character of the community is a great source of pride for Erambie people. Unquestionably, stories of responses to racism are used as group, family and individual identities are developed. Still, these identities are equally built on confirmation of connections to recent and distant histories independent of contact with non-Indigenous people.

A study

My main concern regarding the deficit discourse about Aborigines is that it takes part of a story for the entire story. This does not reflect my experiences living at a mission community. Therefore, one of my goals in writing part of Erambie's oral history tradition is to paint a picture of how senior men and women at Erambie teach an alternative to deficit thinking through storytelling. To do this, stories are treated as research material. My method of collecting information mimics closely the oral history tradition that I grew up with.

The key person in this study is my mother, Mavis. It was Mavis who negotiated my access to the conversations she has with her peers. There is a process for gaining access to oral history at Erambie, and Mavis' support and knowledge of this process was invaluable in recording an authentic representation of the community's oral history tradition.

Certain men and women (born between 1922 and 1950) became key informants and at times acted as co-researchers. Along with Mavis, the Storyteller, Sylvia and Hazel, June, Margaret and Millie shared their stories and facilitated access to group discussions. These key people approved and sponsored my study of the community's oral history tradition (Ritchie 1995). In some instances, I was even told when and where people would be available to meet with me. These sponsors drew their peers (Jean and Joyce) into the project and invited younger men (Brian and Darcy) and women (such as Norma) into the conversation. Others have previously talked about the community elsewhere and some of their stories are used in this book.

This cooperative approach is comparable to the teaching method I am familiar with. Simply asking a question often resulted in a trip around the community as people contributed what they knew about a topic and directed me to other people who 'would know about that'. Discussions often ended with an instruction to 'go and see so and so, they'll be able to tell you about that'. In this way knowledge was imparted by members of the community who were drawn in to act as teachers.

In some instances access to conversations was incidental as I collected them during my normal daily routine. I often took advantage of chance meetings to inform and update people about my study. Consequently, information was obtained in a wide variety of settings within the community. For example, one man offered information about his grandfather during a chance meeting at a local rugby league match in 2004. Others discussed their knowledge of community history in cherry orchards or vineyards while working. In fact, few of the conversations were conducted outside of what I would call my normal routine. Even the arranged meetings were conducted at the homes of community members that I regularly visited for a yarn.

In contrast to this willingness to share their memories, some community members were not initially keen to share or even allow access to their collections of photographs. This reluctance no doubt stems from the practice of stealing photographs, which appears to be common within the community. When I did ask for access I was often confronted by angry older women who jealously guarded their tins full of treasured old photos. In fact, for many people their collection of photographs was their most treasured material possession. Support from Mavis, Millie, June, the Storyteller and Margaret secured access to many photograph collections.

Photographs were used with newspaper clippings, drawings and official records such as birth, death and marriage certificates to jog memories. This was particularly effective and considerable time was spent going through my collection and commenting on what I had uncovered. People often remembered events and details based on this collection. The use of birth, death and marriage certificates is an excellent example of this. Hours were spent recalling relationships between various people and sharing memories.

Even the small sample of photographs I have included adds an enormous amount of information to this book. These photographs are not the result of sociological photography as described by Harper (2004). Rather, they are family photographs that have become tools in knowledge construction even though they may not initially have been composed that way. Still, I have presented these photographs as subjective statements rather than objective documents (Harper 2004). The reader will create a mental picture of the people and places within the community. For example, it is much easier to create a detailed mental picture when a photograph of the railway gates site is included alongside a description. The same is true of certain influential people and teams such as the community football team. I felt this was important because my experience has shown me that many non-Indigenous people rely on stereotypical media images when picturing an Indigenous community and the description I am giving is often in direct contrast to these stereotypical images.

Even though I did want to tell stories using the format that I was familiar with from within my community, I regret that I have not been able to achieve this aim in a way that I can be completely satisfied with. Toward the end of the writing phase of this study I had a conversation with Gamilaroi teacher, Laurie Crawford, that led me to rethink the compromises that I had made to tell this story to outsiders. The conversation provided some comfort for my unease with the choices I had made. Crawford commented that, while some people were preoccupied with the structure of the story and valued linear progression in structuring their stories, 'us blackfellas don't tell stories in a straight line, we go all the way around it'. It has been a continuing source of frustration that I have in a sense given in to writing for general and academic audiences.

The challenge I faced was squeezing the free and wandering yarning tradition of my people into the straight-line (focused) format of academic writing that was acceptable to both of my main audiences. In academic writing the words used to make a story are usually placed in a way that gives the story a structure familiar to white audiences. On the other hand, some Indigenous people will no doubt expect to see a story that they can relate to, a story told the way our people tell it. The answer, or at least part of an answer to this problem of clashing styles, was to make use of photographs.

What I want the reader to keep in mind is that photographs allow an Indigenous storyteller some flexibility to diverge from the straight-line way of telling a story. The pictures in this research have been used in a number of ways. For example, I watched as an Erambie woman used one photograph of the Erambie Allblacks football team to tell a number of stories about the people and events of her youth. She noted a number of related points about the team before detailing family connections and relationships between the players and the community. The picture was also used as a marker of time. 'This picture was taken not long before he died,' she remembered while pointing to one of the players. A child's birth was also dated using the picture, before a detailed description of clothes-washing days at the river was offered in reaction to the unwashed look of one player's uniform. The photograph was used to tell a story in a way that could not be described as a straight line. While I am bound by the conventions of writing to tell a straight-line story, the reader should be aware that it is not the way it is done by Erambie's storytellers. Including photographs is my way of staying true to our way of telling yarns.

Newspaper articles relating to the Erambie Allblacks football team prompted many memories that filled in gaps in the story of the team. In another instance a timeline of the boxing career of an influential community member facilitated discussions about him. Recollections were remarkably accurate. One woman recalled a newspaper article about an athlete practically verbatim fifty years after she had read it. I took this as an indication of the strength of her ability as an oral historian.

Slicaa et al. (1998) suggest that group interviews can be more in keeping with culturally appropriate ways of communicating. More formal interviews have been assessed to be 'too rigid' to work in Indigenous communities (Godwell 1997: 36). While I do find much merit with group discussions, there was no evidence that the Wiradjuri participants in this study were unable to participate in a range of interview types. Sylvia had some experience with formal interviews and she began directing me on the 'proper way' to conduct an interview.

Due to my familiarity with his stories, one-on-one conversations with the Storyteller do not reveal much new information. However, when he was able to participate in group discussions with his peers he switched into performance mode and a great deal of new information resulted. In contrast, some people were more comfortable in one-on-one conversations. Mavis mostly observed when groups were talking. She always made a point of adding her views later in one-on-one discussions.

Group discussions are consistent with the norms of the storytelling tradition rather than a violation of it as the interview process can sometimes be (Slicaa et al. 1998). With my focus on knowledge construction, observing the way these discussions unfolded was at times as valuable as the stories being told. At times, the Storyteller, Margaret and June initiated and guided group conversations that were similar to countless others I have witnessed them lead. I observed how they fed off each other's memories and personalities to reach an agreed version of the community history.

Jim, Hazel, the Storyteller, June and Margaret all have claims to authority over certain areas of knowledge. One of their conversations gave some insight into the way knowledge about community history is negotiated. At times they disagreed in good-natured arguments and made corrections of what they perceived to be each other's mistakes. Jim was, at the time, the oldest man in the community. He was also the oldest living member of the Murray family and was, in his own words, the 'rightful descendant' of the Wiradjuri leader Harry Murray senior. This gave Jim the lion's share of power within the group and on most occasions the others deferred to him.

In this instance, Jim's sisters were also present. They have reputations as community historians and they assert their knowledge with due deference to Jim. The Storyteller, who revelled in the conversation, also has authority within the group, which he 'proved' on a number of occasions during the discussion by displaying his knowledge and the strength of his memory. Although they all established their right to speak, the most boisterous and animated — the Storyteller — guided the discussion while making repeated attempts to show proper respect to Jim. He continually enquired whether Jim needed anything done and was comfortable, and sought his opinions by adding with a cheeky smile, 'as my elder', a number of times. This insight into the way knowledge is constructed within the community proved to be invaluable as I made comparisons between the way Aborigines are represented inside and outside the community.

I idolise Jim and always observed him closely. He was a physically impressive man, being significantly taller than many in the community, and he carried himself in a way that made him seem even taller. He walked with purpose, shoulders back, chest out and chin up at all times. Whenever Jim was in the community he was shown the proper amount of respect for his position as a significant community elder. When he entered a room he became the focus of attention and I found myself in awe of him. Given my own lack of focus when Jim was around, the assistance given by other community members to guide discussion with him was much appreciated. Luckily, the Storyteller took control of the discussion by asking questions and as Jim answered I heard rare insights into life on Erambie from the only man in the community born before the Aborigines Protection Board managers were appointed.

In presenting the stories in this book I want to stick closely to the way I experience the storytelling that inspires my interest. Wherever possible I include quotes that may in some small way give the reader an indication of the way stories are told within the Erambie community.

Some Indigenous historians have wondered whether our history should continue to be passed down only through oral history methods (Taylor 1992). However, Erambie elders do not express this opinion and enthusiastically supported my efforts to record our community's oral history tradition in a written form. Although I do take Taylor's point that recording oral history in this way potentially weakens the oral history tradition, my position is that it is better to record our history using these methods than to risk losing it.

There is one final comment I want to make about the way stories are told in this book. The repetition that characterises storytelling at Erambie did not translate well in written format. Therefore, there is some loss when oral history tradition, even as it incorporates relatively new technologies such as photography, is reproduced in written form. While we do lose some of the divergent meandering characteristics of the spoken word, this is balanced by Sylvia's reminder of the importance of the stories themselves, 'our people have always been great yarners. They would sit under a gum tree and talk and I think we inherited that. Our stories are our survival' (Ingram 2003: 137).

Our Stories

Erambie is, as Norma says, a 'very social' place where people enjoy spending time together yarning. There is idle talk about the mundane of everyday life, current affairs, politics and community gossip that is interrupted by more serious discussions about people and events of the past. Conversations are playful, dramatic, suspenseful and emotional, thought provoking and lyrical. Encounters with the Wiradjuri spirit dog, the *Mirrihula*, are spoken of in hushed tones and stories about *birricks* (ghosts) and the mischievous *gooligahs* (leprechaun-like creatures) are repeated. Instances of racism and prejudice are talked about as one part of a greater repertoire of stories that fits within a wider yarning tradition. Relationships are constantly explained, validated and maintained. Togetherness is the underlying lesson in the stories.

Gossiping about everyday events takes place alongside more formal teaching. Storytelling is often a performance where one or more people, usually community elders, perform one of the stories in their collection. Although there is a difference between yarning among peers and the performances of storytelling, the two types of communication are used interchangeably.

Stories often focus on fulfilling the important task of establishing and maintaining connections to the past, connections to people and places being what Norma calls 'the anchor of the strength of your identity, of who you are'. Men primarily talk about the abilities and achievements of individuals. They debate about the best fighter, swiftest runner, the deadliest football player or singer. While the women also discuss these topics, they talk more generally about the community.

They all talk about learning to value community togetherness from their elders. They are quick to encourage idle children to organise games of 'skippies' or rounders (pronounced 'roundies' by Erambie people) because they are games that the entire community can participate in. As an adult, Josie initiated and participated in games of skipping. She remembered ensuring that all interested people were included in the games because 'that's the way my elders taught me to play'. For Millie the togetherness fostered in these games is a treasured memory from her youth (Read 1984b: 139).[2] Norma remembered, 'we'd be out playing until nightfall and you'd hear the parents all singing out to the kids to come home. We'd be playing rounders. It was really good social interaction and we all grew up as one family'. Norma describes life on the reserve, where there was only one communal water tap and little in the way of material wealth, as 'fantastic'.

Descriptions of Wiradjuri games from the pre-mission era support the women's comments about togetherness being important to Wiradjuri people (Haagen 1994). In 1889 Beveridge described the community involvement in skipping games among the Riverina clans: 'Another favourite amusement of theirs is the skipping rope...As it is being swung round and round the skippers jump in one after another, until there will be as many as a dozen skipping away at once' (in Haagen 1994: 87). The women encourage a sense of togetherness in the games they organise on the mission. They talk about encouraging this togetherness in a way that connects them to the past. They also retell Wiradjuri stories in a way that emphasises connections to the past.

Stories about Wiradjuri legends (Wiradjuri stories) are passed down through generations. Most of the focus is on legends with important messages. Warnings about the dangers posed by the bunyip in the Lachlan River and the *Mirrihula* on the mission after dark are given regularly. Others such as the *gooligah* stories are used as warnings to children. *Gooligah* stories tell of mischievous little people who lurk in dark places ready to cause trouble.

A story about the *buggenj* is told to frighten children into behaving and staying inside after dark. There is little that will engender fear in a Wiradjuri child like a threat that '*buggenj* is out there'. An early observer of Wiradjuri people recorded an encounter with the *buggenj* in 1901:

> Beggeen is the name of one of their evil spirits, or one of the enemies of man; he is supposed to be travelling about the earth, he is heard but not seen. When the aborigines hear a noise in the tops of the trees which sounds like 'Theloo Theloo', they say Beggeen is near, and all collect together in their camp. I have heard the noise myself on several occasions, but could never discover what made it, although I have spent many hours endeavouring to do so. The aborigines are very frightened when they hear the noise, and immediately rush into camp. (Maguire 1901: 88)

One of the more popular stories among Wiradjuri parents, the *Mirrihula* story, has also been told to generations of Wiradjuri children. Mavis tells a story about the *Mirrihula*:

> When I was growing up on Erambie there was story told by my ancestors to all the children to frighten them and keep them inside at night. The Maryhula [sic] dog is about two lovers. There was a young girl and a young man who were in love. However, the girl was promised to an older man. The younger man fought and killed the older man. The young man was then banished from the tribe. If you walk around the camp at night, you will see the Maryhula dog on the outskirts of the camp changing in to the form of a man. (Bamblett et al. 1995)

Senior women in the community take on much of the responsibility for teaching family genealogies. Margaret, born in 1935, points out that the importance of storytelling on the topic is that 'they'll know who they are when you tell them, because they don't know and no one tells them they'll never know who they are'. Margaret also points out that the importance of teaching genealogies is to maintain connections to people and places as well as ensuring correct marriages take place. Ensuring marriages are correct is an important task carried out through storytelling. Without this knowledge connections are lost and incorrect marriages may happen.

Connections to people of the distant past, the 'ancestors', are also constantly reaffirmed in the Wiradjuri stories. The stories that warn of danger posed by the spirits that live in rivers illustrate this point. Mavis tells a story about how Wiradjuri people had a fear of swimming at night passed down to them by their ancestors. It was said that people who swam at night would vanish as the bunyip 'got them'. She added, 'my ancestors [also] had a saying about the Lachlan River at Cowra. They said if you drink from the Lachlan River where the snakes grow bigger you will always come back to the Lachlan River'.

Ethel's parents told her a story that she passed on to her children about the *gidgewa*. The *gidgewa* story is told to warn young children to behave. Another popular story is that the willy-wagtail and curlew birds deliver messages to Wiradjuri people. Gus remembers his Ngunnawal grandmother telling him that she often received messages from a curlew bird days before a telegram arrived to deliver bad news.

June recalled Wiradjuri language being spoken fluently by elders at Erambie and stories being passed on that were 'part of my history' to 'hand down' so younger generations could 'carry it on'. June's grandparents 'used to stand together and talk the language, go for it and I used to be really inquisitive and I'd stand there listening to them…and they'd laugh and all I'd hear was, "*Gootha* [child], she's really interested in what we are saying". One day I said to Granny, teach me to talk like that and she said, "you're too old now". She tried me, couldn't even get my tongue around it'. June added that it was forbidden for Wiradjuri to teach 'the language' on the mission but that her grandparents defied the rule and spoke Wiradjuri openly. June also talks about Wiradjuri rituals and beliefs relating to death, Wiradjuri medicines and other ways that continued on from what she referred to as 'tribal part' of our cultural history.

There are stories that reaffirm the existence of clever men. Darcy, born in 1952, shares a story told to him by a highly regarded Erambie elder:

> I remember this old man whose name was Callaghan and he told me this story. Now Callaghan was a drover of sheep and one day he was taking a mob of sheep from Forbes to Cowra on an outback track right out in the middle of nowhere when he came across this old full-blood man who was sitting on the side of the road. So Callaghan started to talk to him and he then decided to make camp and invited this old man to have something to eat with him. The old man asked him where he was going to and Callaghan told him that he was going to the mission at Cowra. The old man then said that he would have the billy on for him at the mission gates when he got there. So anyway the next morning when Callaghan got up to go on his way the old man was still asleep so Callaghan left him asleep and just went on his way. Now Callaghan was travelling for a week before he got to the mission gates and to his surprise the old man was there at the mission gates with the billy on. The only thing that passed Callaghan and his mob of sheep was a whirly wind. So how do you think the old man got there before him?

Norma remembered her mother's brothers were 'always telling yarns' about Wiradjuri spirits and legends. Mavis too recalled the great yarners of her youth such as Billy and Moodie Merritt who drew people into discussions and jokes around shared fires. The love and enjoyment of teaching within the community is contrasted with the 'cold school' where Mavis says she was taught 'how Captain Cook discovered Australia and the capital letters. Captain Cook, Cook, Cuckoo, that's all they knew. We knew that much about Captain Cook. Dad said to tell that bloody teacher that we were here before Captain Cook'.

Senior men and women discuss connections between current events, people and the recent and distant past every day. Frank Simpson, a community elder, passed on stories about Wiradjuri games played during his childhood and how he had performed a corroboree as a young man. Frank's knowledge of the 'old ways' is often spoken about when the men discuss the songs they were taught by their elders.

Frank, a noted painter, taught many songs to children at Erambie. He learned the song 'Jacky-Jacky' from another Koori man, years before. The

'Jacky-Jacky' song is used within the community to teach and entertain. In addition to 'Jacky-Jacky' and 'Possum Pie', the male elders composed and performed songs such as 'Down the Lachlan River'. The songs are now passed down with stories that are part family history and part community history. Johnno Carroll composed and performed the song 'Down the Lachlan River' when he lived on the Lachlan River bank near Erambie in the 1930s. The song is taught today along with a story about how Carroll had lived at the Railway Bridge camp away from the intrusion of the managers, of how he shared his tent with relatives and gave it away when he moved from the camp. It is also explained that Carroll's daughter, a noted musician and singer herself, had inherited her father's musical ability. 'It's in her blood,' was how Josie and Mavis put it. In addition to telling me the lyrics of the song, Josie described the physical layout of and life within the Railway Bridge camp.

Harry Williams and his brothers grew up alongside the Storyteller at Erambie in the first half of the twentieth century. At the time Harry's father 'Knocker' Williams, Frank Simpson, Johnno Carroll and others were composing and singing songs to entertain themselves and their families. Harry and his brothers became 'black stars' of the national Indigenous music scene as adults (Walker 2000: 167). Successes that the Williams family achieved in the entertainment industry are often the subject of conversation. Margaret linked Harry's talent for music to their uncle, Major Murray. She says, 'Uncle Major had all the boys which he reared, the Williams boys, they could all play an instrument, the whole lot of the boys, really good singers'. Harry's wife Wilga recounted what Harry had told her about his background in music. Williams' story about a night of dance and music staged in one of the red huts (original mission houses) is one that is often told to explain his musical ability:

> Harry was brought up with music. In their day, they entertained themselves. They had this one big night, he told me, in this house like a shed, all the walls opened up, and so word got out, and all the whitefellas used to sit on the boundary and listen. Harry could play any sort of string instrument you'd like [to] stick in his hand. Him and his uncles and his father. They used to make costumes out of old hessian bags. (Walker 2000: 167)

Harry's contemporary musical ability is linked to that of his ancestors by a non-Indigenous observer. The reference to the ability of mimics is comparable to the way Erambie storytellers refer to Williams' ancestors when discussing his singing:

> Harry Williams in striped sneakers and painters cap, wife Wilga and the country Outcasts continue a seemingly endless string of songs and jokes. Early settlers here found to their dismay that the Australians could mimic any sound they heard, from dingo's howl to Scottish brogue. Hearing the Outcasts imitate that American nasal C&W twang, you can appreciate the settlers' alarm. But Australia has its own country style and sound too, and the Outcasts are real flash characters. But they still retain the same inexpressible, unpretentious, uninhibited love of expression that circumvents self-consciousness and leaves the senses — so neatly glad-wrapped today by premeditated stage acts — stunned and humming with renewed sense of (Ab)originality. (Walker 2000: 180)

Williams' family are known generally within the community for their ability as entertainers. When the topic of music comes up in conversations the link to the recent past (family members) and the distant past (unnamed Wiradjuri ancestors) is made once more. Williams' performance is described in a way that is similar to a *Cowra Free Press* description of a performance during which his father and other family members 'had the audience in roars of laughter' (1 August 1930). Connections are made between family members through stories that begin with, 'I'll tell you who could sing', or, 'by gees, that Knocker Williams [Harry's father] could play music on anything'. The way that Harry Williams and his brothers are spoken about leaves no doubt that Erambie people believe their abilities to entertain was 'in their blood'. All of Harry's children are thought to have inherited his musical ability. In some instances the present (for example, people's abilities) is connected to the past by implication. Recognition of Harry Williams' musical abilities will be followed by a story of his parents' talents as performers. At other times the connection is explicitly made.

June remembers Harry's brother Boomanulla telling great tales, 'he made them up, a lot of stories you know, mainly about country and western and that and he'd tell these stories and have us lying real quiet listening. Perhaps a scary one, you know'. June's memories of Boomanulla became part of the storytelling tradition that he helped pass on to her. June said that storytelling is 'being educated'. It was Harry who reminded June that 'we've come from a very proud race of people and they were strong…Dignified people'. June adds, 'that's what I keep telling my son' how 'strong' and 'good' the people (her elders) from the mission were. June's words here sum up the essence of storytelling at Erambie. Young people are educated about the strength to be found in a sense of community and the beauty of Wiradjuri culture.

Life on the reserve was not always idyllic and the community's repertoire of stories also includes descriptions of instances of racism. Erambie people talk about racism in a number of ways. Some stories are told in an off-hand, almost detached manner while others bring out strong emotional responses decades after the events took place. Mavis gives some indication of the way racism intruded on her everyday life when she says in a matter-of-fact tone, 'racism was really bad. People of Erambie had a lot of barricades put up against them'. Stories of children being taken away are common. Mavis frequently tells the following story with bitterness:

> When the police came for them, they surrounded the house. He [the manager] had three or four police with him. The police came and took them. They surrounded the house, so they couldn't run away. I still remember the day they took them. I was upset. They were about my age. He was standing right at the door then, the manager, making sure they didn't get away. Then she [Shirley] brought them out, she had them all dressed and clean, and they took them away. She had to move out of the house. That's the only way he could get back at her when she beat him in court. Isobel, Matty, Fanny, Colly, Dinky…I was there when they took them. Mum Shirl [Shirley], she was minding them kids and she never neglected the kids, she looked after them. The manager…said the kids were neglected. Those kids weren't neglected, they was well looked after. I think they stayed in the homes until they was old enough to come out too. Fanny, Matty, Isobel, Dinky, Colin, he took them. I still remember the day they took them. He's [the manager] probably burning in hell for what he done.

Mavis added that one of the reasons people moved regularly was as a strategy to combat the threat of children being removed:

Before my time I think they used to go and hide with the kids. And they travelled a lot. Nan used to travel, she'd go from here to Griffith, you know, she'd never stayed too long. That was the reason, they didn't want to stay too long in one place because of the Welfare. That's one reason they moved around.

Sylvia remembered that segregation in the town even extended to the local hospital:

They used to have segregation here in Cowra…They [Cowra hospital] had a ward out the back. Further down the back they had a ward for the Kooris and that's where they used to put us, and the women, when they had their babies. That's where they went and everything was marked A.B.O. Napkins, bedpans, sheets, everything was segregated.

The incidences of racism were contrasted with some examples of white people who were considered friends of the community. Mavis recounted an often-told story about a local doctor who was known for her angry rejection of racist attitudes within the town:

The hospitals and the ambulance drivers talked about the kids and the people going to hospital dirty, it was mostly winter time they got sick. There was a doctor, Enid McLaren, she told the nurses and the ambulance drivers that if they had to wash in cold water in the middle of winter, they would be dirty too. She spoke up for Erambie people until they got the electricity on.

Mostly the stories about racism deal with the intrusion of the Aborigines Welfare Board and its predecessor on the everyday lives of the people on the mission. There is particular resentment of the removal of children, household inspections and rationing of food. The following stories about the role of the managers and the injustices they were responsible for give some indication of how outsiders intruded on the lives of Erambie people. Esther gave a general account of the role of the managers during her childhood:

When we grew up you had to live under the manager's rules here… The managers had the authority to stop people from coming into the mission, or bar them from leaving there…I don't think that anyone would want the managers back. (in Rimas-Kabaila 1996: 21)

Stories make it clear that the mission residents exercised power in their relationships with outsiders. Women often refused entry when the matron attempted to carry out inspections and men angrily confronted managers whenever they attempted to stand over them or their family members. For example, Josie delights in telling a story about her older sister leaving a welfare officer standing at the front door for some time before sending him a message to 'make an appointment' when he wanted to visit her at home. Battles with the managers are prominent in the stories that are told about this aspect of mission life. Matilda sums up how community elders viewed the intrusion of the managers:

> They found the constant supervision from the manager and his wife was just too much for people who were used to living without someone breathing down their necks. It really irritated my father I think right up 'til the day he died. He just couldn't stand that supervision from whites, because he was a very proud man. (in Read 1984b: 76)

Respected elders Ethel and Pearl assessed managers harshly. Ethel's assessment of the managers was that 'there've been some good ones and some bad ones', although her final judgement was that they were 'all the same' in the end (in Read 1984b: 71–2). Pearl also judged the managers and their wives harshly because they would 'go right in and out through your home to see if it was clean' (in Read 1984b: 31). The stories Ethel and Pearl told are representative of the way that managers are viewed at Erambie. When the elders talk about the 'managers' days' the listener is left in no doubt about the resentment they feel about their presence on the mission.

Some Wiradjuri and Ngunnawal words were given new meaning to reflect new experiences. The managers relied on the police and local courts to enforce their authority. When the role of the police is described, an explanation of the term *burramaldine* is included. *Burramaldine* means 'someone who grabs another' and it is explained that the police were given this name because it characterises their relationship with people at Erambie. Mavis explains:

> You'd see them coming and you'd sing out and they'd run. Run to get off the mission. The kids used to hide from the *gunyans* [another word for police]. They thought they were gonna take em away see, welfare, *gunyans* was coming to get them. When they'd come on the mission

everybody would sing out, '*burramaldine!*' and you wouldn't see many people then. Yeah, to grab, '*burramaldine!*' they'd sing out.

When the managers came to Erambie they brought with them a system of rationing government-provided food. The managers were responsible for administering the ration system and community elders often talk about the injustices of the way they did this. Josie made the following comments about the rations:

> You want to know about rations? Yeah, they gave them out to us. Bread, little brown paper bags of sago: sago, tea, sugar, they were in little brown paper bags. They used to call them half a pound then I think it was half a pound. Men used to work for them, they'd go and work for the rations, do two days' work. Women used to work over at the manager's house. Help the matron, clean her house out and that, they'd work two hours for her for the rations. The girls was supposed to help in the treatment room, supposed to go in there for two days. But she'd take two girls over there and clean her house up…They'd go in the office and leave us in there cleaning up their dirty house, doing their house work. It was only a little bit [the ration of food], and some of the stuff they wouldn't eat, it was treacle, marmite. Some of the stuff wasn't even eatable. That sago, they wouldn't eat that much.

Despite the recollections of negative experiences with racism, community elders' memories remain overwhelmingly positive when discussing the past. For June it was the 'wonderful sense of humour' of Wiradjuri people that helped them deal with the intrusions from the Aborigines Protection Board. June focused more on the togetherness of the community and the happy times shared at Erambie:

> Uncle Major, they'd get me to get him to come and play for a dance. The kids would say, "go on, Uncle Major will do it for you". Every time he'd say, "sing me a song first". I had to sing a song before he'd agree. But they [adults] had us singing and dancing. They had big dances in the houses…we'd have to get up and dance with the old boys. They'd dance with us and they taught us all to dance…We did everything together, the activities that went on. Dances, we all come together and had those dances.

Despite all the resentment at bad treatment, Mavis' generation still retains fond memories of life on the mission. Mavis resented attempts to control her grandmother, '[she] was a tribal woman. She used to travel around, they followed the tribal laws when they could'. Still, despite the intrusions, Mavis' stories about life on the mission paint a picture of an ideal community life. For her the community was a positive place due to 'people, the people that lived there, the people. The people. It was the people'. Josie also remembers her childhood during the managerial era as a happy time because of this focus on community:

> If anyone had more than anyone else they would share. I remember if someone had a little kerosene they would help two or three houses with the one little bottle of kero. If they had made any soup they would share the soup and bread with a family that had nothing at the time. We did the same with all the rations — soap, tea, sugar, flour. Not like the white people, we shared what we had. All we would have to do is ask our aunties and the aunties would make sure that no family went without. Life seemed to revolve around the women, they were the backbone of our community. You never went to the men to ask for things, always the women. They were the boss of running the household and held things together. Even though many of the women were not my real aunties, out of respect we referred to them all as aunts. My aunties were just great and I always remember the love and kindness they showed to me and to one another…I have many fond memories of life at Erambie.

There are many stories that echo these sentiments about the role of community elders in maintaining a sense of community. Functions on the riverbank are likened to corroborees even though dancers moved to contemporary songs such as the 'Shanghaied Rooster' and 'Jacky-Jacky'. Tunes were played on gum leaves and spoons. The meanings attached to a corroboree were retained even as people attended dances at Erambie's community hall and declared, in European terms, that they would 'swing Jessie tonight'. For June, life on Erambie during the 1930s to 1940s was 'the good old days [when] we were all sharing'. June cherishes the memories of togetherness and the 'communal' way of living that made her feel 'protected'. Given their positive experiences, it is not surprising that Erambie elders angrily reject assimilation as a policy for future development. June blamed 'mainstream living' for 'breaking down our people'.

Stories are used every day to teach and entertain people. However, their most important use may be as a form of community unifier. People come together on a daily basis to gossip and keep up to date with community and wider current affairs and events. Senior men and women make sure connections are reaffirmed to the past through storytelling about Wiradjuri legends as well as connections to people such as the leaders, athletes, singers and musicians that are important to the community. People yarning at Erambie are telling stories about togetherness. They are following our elders' teaching. The storytelling and oral history tradition is an important part of the culture lived every day by Erambie people. Erambie's storytelling tradition is itself continuity of culture.

Chapter 3

The famous Erambie Allblacks

'An octoroon is a long way from being a white man.' (*Cowra Free Press* 16 August 1923)

After the end of the football season, when Erambie Allblacks won the cup, there was dancing for three or four weeks.
(Smith & Sykes 1981: 12)

The Erambie Allblacks rugby league team played a significant role in establishing and continuing representations of Aborigines.[1] Erambie football players were represented in a way that was consistent with racial thought of their time. At the same time, the Allblacks' story illustrates the use of a European sport within an Indigenous community as an example of adaptation and retention of important aspects of pre-invasion culture. Members of the team were known differently by black and white communities during the 1920s through to the 1940s. The local newspapers represented the Allblacks through the stereotypes and anxieties of the local white communities, and these representations varied according to the state of race relations across Wiradjuri country. In contrast, Erambie senior men and women remember the team as an example of Wiradjuri culture being continued.

The game for racehorses

Cowra newspapers reported Wiradjuri men Harry and Sam Murray playing rugby football from the turn of the twentieth century. In 1908 a group of Sydney sporting identities and disenfranchised rugby union players formed a breakaway football competition. Administrators of the new game planned an aggressive marketing strategy that included rule changes that promised a more spectacular and open style of play. The 'game for race horses', rugby league, was promoted as entertainment for the working classes and the Sydney sporting journal *The Referee* wrote that the new form of football was preferred by spectators (in Heads 1992: 18). The rugby league historian Ian Heads has suggested that there was a special relationship between the game and people in rural areas:

> The very essence of rugby league exists in the 'bush' in the ancient and enduring image of young men pulling on boots and rough jumpers and heading out onto a cleared patch to play the winter game. (1992: 103)

By 1912, Western District towns such as Bathurst had taken up rugby league. During what Heads called the second and more pronounced wave of growth, rugby league reached further west to Cowra in 1920.

Articles in the 1920 *Cowra Free Press* (hereafter *CFP*) suggest that Herbert 'Doolan' Murray was the first man from Erambie to play rugby league and that he was followed by a number of Erambie men into Cowra's league teams in 1920 and 1921. In 1922, the people of Erambie formed a team of their own.

The team was organised by Harry Murray senior, and his son Doolan captained them. Mavis remembered Doolan Murray as a small, athletic man. In 1922 he was also building a reputation as a boxer. He had a knockout punch that she said he hid behind a constant smile and jovial nature. Doolan was joined in the team by his equally gifted brothers, Frank 'Bully' Broughton and Harry 'Major' Murray. The Storyteller talked about Major Murray's athleticism when he recalled him doing back-flips and catching footballs mid-flight to entertain children at Allblacks' training. Eventually, all six of the Murray brothers played for the team. They were joined by Dave Perry, Ernest 'Buffalo' Whitty, Paul 'Callaghan' Coe and John Charles. According to the Storyteller, Robert Carroll senior, his brother Stanley Carroll and James 'Cutter' Bamblett were tall heavy men known for their serious no-nonsense nature and strength. Robert Carroll and Bamblett led the forward pack while the musically gifted brothers Alf 'Knocker' Williams and Lachlan 'Diamond' Ingram played a number of backline positions. Together, this group of men were the core of the team for more than a decade.

On Sunday 25 June 1922 the Erambie Allblacks played their first game against the Cowra Pioneers. The *CFP* included the following report on the match:

> A team of footballers from Erambie Mission and a Pioneer team provided a very interesting game on Sunday, which was full of thrills, the speed and tackling of the aboriginals being a revelation, and when they become more conversant with the rules they will be hard to beat. The game resulted in a win for the Pioneers by 16 to 14. The Murray brothers were the pick of the losers. (28 June 1922)

In the years leading up to 1922 there were occasional articles about Aborigines in the *CFP*. However, the introduction of the Erambie football team into the local sporting scene coincided with an increase in the number of articles about Aborigines. The team seems to have become a focal point for representations of Aborigines. Articles consistently presented Aborigines as inferior to whites while, at the same time, emphasising their animal-like athleticism. In the first article on the team, for example, the language focused on the physical attributes of the Erambie team. Nine days before the Allblacks first match a *CFP* article claimed black cultures were inferior and that 'the white man is superior' (17 June 1922). In the context of this type of racial thinking, it is perhaps not difficult to see why the athletic ability of the Erambie men may have been 'a revelation'.

When the Allblacks and Pioneers met again the result was another loss for the Erambie team. Although they lost, the team impressed the sports reporter from the *CFP* who again noted their athletic ability:

> The game between the Pioneers and the coloured men from Erambie was fast and exciting from start to finish. At half-time the blacks led 2 0 and the spectators were roused to a high pitch of enthusiasm. Not for some time has such barracking been heard on the Cowra ground. The tackling of the blacks was a revelation, the Murray brothers and Stanley being particularly deadly. (5 July 1922)

The Allblacks third and final match of their first season, according to the *CFP* was another loss against the Pioneers (19 July 1922). Despite Major Murray's two tries, the Allblacks lost narrowly — as had been the case in their two previous meetings — perhaps only due to inaccurate goal kicking. After this match the *CFP* continued to include articles that focused on race. For example, one article justified 'guarding a white Australia' against all other races. A quote from the article draws a picture of one strand of racial thinking at the time:

The ideal Australia of the future is a land populated from north to south by a diversity of prosperous white producers living in a high state of civilisation...Against the penetration of lower standard of life producers of this type provide the cheapest and most effective garrison. (20 September 1922)

Drawing the colour line

Western District rugby league was not organised into regular competitions in the 1920s. Instead, matches were played on a challenge basis where team secretaries issued challenges through either direct correspondence or the local newspapers. During this early period newspapers were integral in the promotion of the emerging game. As rugby league gained increasing exposure, individuals began to sponsor cups that usually bore their names. Perhaps the best-known cup competition in country rugby league was the Maher Cup. However, a successful team could have a number of cups in their possession. According to newspaper reports, at the beginning of the 1923 football season the Cowra Pioneers were the holders of the Cooley, Oxley and Kevin cups.

The Allblacks formed again for the 1923 rugby league season. During their second season the team played more matches, and there was a corresponding increase in the number of newspaper articles that concentrated on race compared to the summer, when football was not played. During the football season that year both the Erambie team and racially oriented stories appeared regularly on the front pages of the *CFP*. During the four-month period of the season, for example, the twice-weekly *CFP* included 21 articles related to Aborigines. The majority of the articles appeared during the periods when the Allblacks challenged the Pioneers. They included stereotypical and derogatory representations of black races. These articles raise the possibility that the matches were meaningful for many locals for reasons beyond mere sport.

The owner of the *CFP* claimed his motto was: 'Pandering to none, yet acting impartially to all' (in Marriott 1988: 104). Stereotypes are sometimes considered to contain an element of truth. For example, Lee, Jussim and McCauley argue that stereotypes are exaggerations of real group differences or that they are often accurate (1995). However, while the newspapers reported actual events such as crimes committed by Aborigines, it is the emphasis on race that contributed to ideas about 'real group differences' that is of interest here. The newspapers did contain articles that reported negative behaviour of both black and white people. However, the language used in reports differed according to the racial background of the subject. For example, when white men were convicted of theft a description of their case and the outcome appeared without any reference to race. On the other hand, when an Aborigine committed a crime his background was the main topic of the report. The language of race used here suggests that popular ideas about race were more important than claims of 'impartiality' in the way Aborigines were represented. As Hall writes: '[t]he press, for better or worse' often 'articulated the insecurity, mixed with fear and loathing, of its readers' (1998: 5).

The Allblacks' first match of 1923 was on 29 May when they played a team from nearby Woodstock. Prior to the match, the *CFP* published a notice that stated: 'The All Blacks have challenged the Pioneers for the Cooley Cup' (25 May 1923). The following report on the Woodstock match is noteworthy because it suggested the Allblacks were beginning to draw the public's attention and interest:

> A fair crowd turned up at the recreation ground on Sunday afternoon, the chief attraction no doubt being to see the All Blacks in action for the first time this season…The All Blacks (the dark complexioned players from Erambie) were opposed to Woodstock whom they defeated after a fast and interesting game by 13 to nil. (29 May 1923)

The Allblacks' challenge to the Pioneers instigated a rivalry that lasted for decades. During this time the *CFP* continued to publish articles that represented Aborigines in a negative way. Many of the articles detailed crimes committed by Aborigines. One such article, headlined 'Half-caste sentenced for attack on school mistress', was published even though the incident did not occur in the Cowra district (5 June 1923). Three days later the following reply from officials of the Pioneers to the Allblacks' challenge was printed in the *CFP*:

> Sir, — The following is a copy of a letter sent to Doolan Murray, sec. of the "All Blacks" regarding a challenge to the Pioneer Football Club,

which appeared in the columns of your paper some little time ago…I as assistant secretary, wish to reply to a challenge for the 'Cooley Cup' from the All Blacks…Firstly one of the rules of our club, formulated at the annual meeting states: That no matches shall be played against the All Blacks (as a team) nor shall membership of the club be open to any of them. Hence, it is impossible for me, as secretary, to accept any such match (Cup or otherwise)…that cup, now being the property of the Pioneers, will be withdrawn from play…So Mr Editor, your many readers will see that unless the rule referred to above be altered, nothing can be done in connection with the challenge. Also, Mr Editor (as an afterthought), I wonder how many of our local so called 'sports' who are so anxious to see this match eventuate would be willing to strip for such a match? I wonder! (8 June 1923)

It is not stated why the Cowra Pioneers had altered their club rules to exclude Aborigines. However, this in itself was not an unusual act. Excluding black athletes or 'drawing the colour line' was common practice in eighteenth and nineteenth century sport (Sailes 1998; Bass 2005; Booth & Tatz 2000; Holt 1989). In this instance, the Pioneers' officials took the decision after local Wiradjuri had been playing members of local football clubs (in the rugby codes) for more than two decades. The only hint of an explanation for the club's change of position comes from the question of the official who asked 'who would be willing [to play Aborigines]'. The implication here is that the Pioneers were not acting outside of community sentiment in excluding Aborigines and the action did not warrant further explanation for this reason. On the other hand, the comment '"sports" who were so anxious to see [the] match' indicates that it may not have been acceptable to all that Aborigines were excluded on the basis of race. The emergence of the Allblacks as a team that represented the Erambie community may have been a threat to the status quo in the racial hierarchy in a way that individual Erambie Aborigines playing in mostly white teams had not. The team collectively was apparently more significant than the individual athletes who had previously competed against white people in the area.

Even though the officials of the Pioneers considered their exclusion of Aborigines to be acceptable within the Cowra community, the matter was discussed further. A week after refusing the Allblacks' challenge, the Pioneers club held another meeting to discuss the issue. At the time these discussions were taking place the *CFP* reported that notorious 'dusky' criminal Roy Governor had fallen 'fighting' the police (12 June 1923). No reasons were given for revisiting the Allblacks issue. However, the *CFP* reported that the Allblacks had some support within the community:

> The vexed question concerning the playing of the All Blacks was brought up and discussed. A motion rescinding a previous one was passed now enabling the club to play the All Blacks. Sunday July 15th has been fixed for the match...A good, fast and exciting game is expected so roll up you All Blacks supporters if you want to get set and settled. (15 June 1923)

In the lead-up to the match, the *CFP* increased the number of articles relating to race. On 6 July three articles were published. The first article was a description of the Allblacks match against a team from nearby Koorawatha:

> Sunday afternoon last was an evening of excitement on the local recreation ground...the next match as between the All Blacks of Cowra and Koorawatha's crack team. This match was at times very exciting: the 'coons' played a very tricky game and scored a decisive victory over Koorawatha by 11 to 3. The Murray–Broughton combination was good to witness...chatting with several of the All Blacks after the match they referred to their future match with the Pioneers, and judging by their talk they seem to be very confident of gaining victory over that team on Sunday week. (6 July 1923)

The second article described how a 'dark skinned resident of Cowra' had been arrested in Orange for threatening to cut his white wife's throat. Also in this edition, an article reported that 'great interest' was being shown in the Allblacks–Pioneers football match. Four days later, the match was mentioned again when readers were reassured that 'the much discussed Pioneers–All Blacks match would definitely take place' (10 July 1923). The match between a team from a community of less than 100 residents and the Pioneers from a town of more than 3000 had been built up to the point that the *CFP* reported:

It might truly be said that never before has so much interest been envinced [sic] in the meeting of two local teams as thus shown in the above fixture set down for next Sunday. The fame of the All Blacks was spread far and wide and they are not lacking in supporters, many of whom are sanguine of their success. But in this writer's opinion the abos will have to show marked improvement...visitors are coming from Greenthorpe, Koorawatha and a record 'gate' is anticipated. (10 July 1923)

The *CFP* article did not reflect on why so much interest had surrounded this match or the paper's own role in building it up. Instead, it continued a narrative which pitched the whites against the blacks. In another article leading up to the match the newspaper noted that a combined 'white' team made up of Pioneers and Rovers players had beaten the 'Coloured men' (26 June 1923). When the Allblacks lost it was usually noted that they had lost to a 'white' team. The reports also mentioned that the Allblacks suffered a big blow in their last lead-up match when their star player Harry 'Major' Murray was injured (6 July 1923). The loss of such an influential player for this important match must have been devastating for a team that already had called on players from the crowd on occasions.

Doolan Murray's son Jim remembered that the site for the match was the West Cowra Recreation ground that had previously been a campsite for local Wiradjuri. The ground was a short walk from Erambie and Jim remembered that a separate entrance had been established for Aborigines. The *CFP* reported that, when the Erambie supporters arrived at the ground, they refused to pay the entrance fee of threepence when they learned that the Pioneers were to receive all the gate money (10 July 1923). Controversy again arose before kick-off as the Allblacks refused to play unless Cowra referee Jim Hyslop was in charge. Finally they got their way and the Allblacks took the field to the roars of their barrackers.

After the match, the *CFP* reporter 'Phair Dinkum' wrote a front-page article which appeared under the headline 'Coloured team decisively beaten':

The long looked forward to match...at the recreation ground on Sunday proved a big draw, over 1000 people being present including 200 residents of the Erambie and Goolagong missions...in the first half, although on the defensive the blacks held their own, their deadly tackling and spoiling tactics a chief feature of the play. The Pioneers only succeeded in breaking through the coloured team's sound defence on one occasion...Pioneers who are a fine body of young athletes, practically all teetotallers and non-smokers invariably reserve their best efforts for the second half...After resumption of play even play followed for a time and the blacks' supporters were jubilant at the showing the abos were making. Eventually L Stammers, securing the ball from a scrum near half way, short punted and again gaining possession, he used his rare pace to full advantage and out pacing the speedy coons, scored behind the posts...the final scores Pioneers 15 Allblacks 2...Owing to the Allblacks, for some unaccountable reason, refusing to play under Mr Poplin of Young, Mr Jim Hyslop refereed and gave general satisfaction...Next Sunday the Pioneers and All Blacks will again meet, when those who when informed by the gate keeper that the Pioneers were to receive the whole of the gate receipts, refused to contribute will be given an opportunity to show whether they were conscientious objectors as the All Blacks are to receive the takings. (10 July 1923)

'Phair Dinkum' clearly differentiates between the 'almost' all 'teetotaller' Pioneers and the 'coons' of the Allblacks. Another article published in this edition further stressed this difference. The front page carried the headline: 'Making merry at the mission, half-caste convicted of drunkenness'. This article described the court case that resulted from an incident where an Erambie resident was charged with being drunk and disorderly. The incident started when a police officer claimed he had 'heard someone shouting' when riding past the reserve. Despite evidence that the noise resulted from the Erambie Allblacks training and that the man was not drunk, the magistrate decided he 'could not place much reliance' on the evidence of Aborigines. When asked by the magistrate why he had not had a lot of charges brought up against Aborigines, the police officer replied: 'they are very hard to catch, there are some very bad characters there at times but they scamper off like mice when the police come.' He added that 'they have no industries and the residents sometimes number 150' (in *CFP* 10 July 1923).

According to the *CFP*, the lack of white control and closeness of the reserve to the town was an issue of concern and some white residents were attempting to pressure the Aborigines Protection Board into relocating the mission away from the town (28 May 1923). It was in this climate that the readers of the *CFP* were told of the lack of 'industry' and the bad character of people on the reserve. The overall impression given by the evidence of the officer was that a dangerous group of people were living close to the town and he could not guarantee he could control them.

The differences between black and white were again reinforced when, in a rematch between Pioneers and the Allblacks, the *CFP* reported that the game resulted in 'rough house' tactics by some of the Allblacks (24 July 1923). The Murray brothers were singled out as 'always good hard tacklers — but never dirty'. The Pioneer's players who were 'not entirely faultless' were excused for they could 'scarcely be blamed for retaliating and paying back'. Three days later an article headlined 'Doubtful doings at dark-town' told how there was a 'want of morals at the Erambie mission' (27 July 1923).

Although it peaked during the periods when the Allblacks challenged the Pioneers, the derogatory tone of articles about Aborigines in the *CFP* continued for decades. Articles with sensational headlines such as 'Booze at Erambie mission' detailed how a 'part Aborigine' was told that 'an octoroon was a long way from being a white man' by the local magistrate (16 August 1923). In a later article a man arrested for being drunk and disorderly was identified as an Aborigine by the headline: 'Offender from Erambie Mission' (7 May 1929). The difference of Aborigines was reinforced constantly in the reports that ranged from subtle mentions of Aborigines' degradation through alcohol to the danger from 'the black menace' and the comical 'Jacky-Jacky' character. The common thread in these stories is the difference between whites and Aborigines, with the inferiority of the Aborigines implied or stated outright.

A bright future may have been expected for the Allblacks after the attention they received from their matches with the local white teams in 1923. However, in 1924 the Allblacks did not play as a team. Instead, many of the players remained active, playing in local teams including the Pioneers. The issue of the Pioneers barring black players would be revisited in the future but in 1924 they welcomed the men from Erambie into their team.

When faced with prejudice and racism, the Allblacks' leadership of Harry and Doolan Murray may have used the public challenge to force the Pioneers to play them and rescind their colour bar. I can only speculate on the amount of support there was for each position. However, the newspaper reports do suggest that there were some objections raised by white people when the Allblacks were excluded. This is consistent with what Jim told me about the close friendships between some white people and people from Erambie and demonstrates the danger of characterising groups of people as racist based on specific examples from documentary sources. The way Aborigines are represented in the *CFP* articles does suggest prejudices existed in the town. However, there is also some evidence that not everyone accepted the negative representations.

Stereotypes and contact

While Allport argued that personal contact changes stereotypes (1954), this contact hypothesis is disputed by Hewstone and Browne's theory that contact leads instead to sub-typing rather than ending stereotypes (1986). It is difficult to know the level of contact between Wiradjuri and the people of Cowra. Oral history from Erambie residents suggests both parties preferred to keep interaction to a minimum. One Erambie resident, Tom, remembered, 'we hardly knew the town was there', and another, Mavis, told me that community elders warned her against going into the town (in Rimas-Kabaila 1996: 19). Sport, and football in particular, may have been one of the few areas where personal contact was made between the communities at this time.

The newspaper reports suggest that the identity of Cowra's white population was partly developed using stereotypical representations of Aborigines. This is consistent with Hinton who has followed the work of Fanon and Said in identifying self-interest as motivation for representing one's own group more favourably than another (Hinton 2000). The basis of Fanon's argument here is that the language used to represent colonised people makes plain the need for the white man to keep the black man 'within bounds' and where he belongs:

I ascribe a basic importance to the phenomenon of language... Every colonised people finds itself face to face with the language of the civilising nation; that is, with the culture of the mother country. The colonised is elevated above his jungle status in proportion to his adoption of the mother country's cultural standards. (Fanon 1952/1970: 14)

Perhaps the most obvious evidence of this comes from the report of the Allblacks–Pioneers match in 1923. According to the *CFP* report, the Pioneers were 'a fine body of young athletes, practically all teetotallers' (10 July 1923). By omission alone, it could be argued that the Allblacks were placed in an opposite category. Furthermore, when contrasted with the 'half-caste convicted of drunkenness' headline that appeared in another article on the same page, the idea that Aborigines were different is reinforced. What emerges is a sense that the representation of the Allblacks was linked to the social identity of white people. It seems fair to suggest that a desire to shape a white identity was part of the motivation for stereotypical reporting of Aborigines.

Competition that lead to hostility and prejudice is another factor that may have contributed to the stereotyped representation of the Allblacks (Sherif & Sherif 1953). Read argued that white people in Cowra sought tighter control of Erambie residents in the early part of the twentieth century. He found that the Aborigines Protection Board appointed a white manager to the Erambie reserve 'as a result of complaints of the people of Cowra' (Read 1983: 71). The following quote from *The wretched of the earth* supports Read's point:

> The colonial world is cut in two…The zone where natives live is not complementary to the zone inhabited by settlers. The two zones are opposed…the native town, the negro village, the medina, the reservation, is a place of ill fame, peopled by men of evil repute. (Fanon 1967: 29–31)

Language is used to establish the inferiority of the people to be colonised and justify ongoing colonisation. Language, therefore, is essential in the process of colonisation.

In fact, people at Erambie say that a manager was appointed as a 'compromise' between Erambie leaders and white authorities who preferred to move the Erambie reserve further from the outskirts of the town, which at the time was expanding to meet the Erambie boundary. This assertion is supported by an article in the *CFP* outlining conflict between Wiradjuri elders and the first white manager of the reserve (28 March 1926). Erambie stood on valuable land overlooking the Lachlan River so the competition between the Allblacks and Pioneers may have represented more than just the boasting rights of football teams. Competition for land may have heightened feelings of animosity between the groups that in turn contributed to the importance of the football matches.

The minimal contact between mission residents and local whites may have increased the power of newspaper stories to influence the way Aborigines were known. Language used to describe Aborigines in the *CFP* was geared toward constructing an identity that is associated with behaviour contrary to the values of a 'civilised' white majority. Drawing on the work of Fanon, Said and Hinton on the way colonised groups are viewed by their colonisers, we can read the Allblacks' challenges to the Cowra Pioneers as representing a threat to existing stereotypes. Reports in the *CFP* were one of the ways that this threat was manifested and managed.

Allblacks versus the Champions

In 1925 the Erambie Allblacks played a match against a team called the Mandurama Reds. The Reds were reputed to be the best rugby league team in country football. This match became a part of the Erambie community's storytelling tradition. The way the Allblacks is represented within the community is an example of continuity of Wiradjuri culture. In addition to representing a continuation of a tradition of storytelling, the stories community members tell about this match suggest a continuation of community socialisation in the story of the Allblacks.

The Mandurama Reds were similar to the Erambie Allblacks in that they came from a relatively small community. However, they were able to keep a group of highly skilled footballers together in the 1920s and 1930s. The *CFP* recorded some of the Reds' achievements:

> The celebrated Mandurama Reds…have a rather fine record. Throughout the lengthy period of four seasons they have only suffered defeat on two occasions…The team apparently specialises in winning cups, for the club holds the following…Blayney Cup, Blayney Citizens'

Cup...Woodstock (Shipp) Cup and Cowra (Ryall and Robinson) Cups and won outright the Blayney (McBeth) Cup, the Blayney (Hordern) Cup and Quinn challenge shield. In addition to having all these trophies, the Reds have won the Blayney competition...it would appear the Reds have a mortgage on the Mandurama Challenge Cup. The Reds can feel justifiably proud of their remarkable record. (9 August 1922)

After the Reds suffered a rare loss (to a representative team) the *Carcoar Chronicle* also heaped praise on them:

The 'Reds' defeated at last but it took a combined district team to do it... possibly no other club in the west has had such an honour conferred upon them. For a club team to be invited by the head officers of the Bathurst league to play combined Bathurst and to have the match boomed as an attraction of the season — which it undoubtedly was — was indeed a compliment to the prowess of the Mandurama team. Although beaten the 'Reds' assuredly added to their fame as players...Mr H. Read, sole selector for the Western District, characterised the 'Reds' as the best club team that has yet visited Bathurst. (15 August 1922)

It is clear from the reports above that the Reds enjoyed a reputation as a champion team. They 'graduated' to playing district teams when they had built their reputation at club level. This is a good indication of the progression available to teams during this period before the establishment of group football competitions. The Reds' reputation as a team is vital to the way the story of the Allblacks is told within our community.

In the lead-up to the match, the Allblacks' own growing reputation as players was being mentioned in the accounts of their matches. 'Phair Dinkum' suggested in the *CFP* that a match between 'the Pioneers and Allblacks would be a greater attraction than other competition offered' (7 July 1925). Some of the Allblacks players were again alternating between playing for their own team and the Pioneers during this season. Major Murray in particular was consistently scoring tries for both teams and the heated rivalry of 1923 had apparently cooled by the 1925 football season. Whichever team they turned out for, the Erambie players were becoming recognised for their ability on the football field. In one match against Koorawatha, for example, the football correspondent to the *CFP* wrote:

Koorawatha first graders are to try conclusions with a team from Erambie mission, the dusky members of which bear a good reputation as players. As most of our senior players have not kicked a ball this season so far, they will have to face a pretty tough proposition when meeting the darkies. (22 May 1925)

In the lead-up to the match the *Carcoar Chronicle* printed the following advertisement on 10 July 1925:

Football!
Mandurama Reds v. Cowra Aboriginals
Sunday July 19, 3 pm
Roll up Roll up
E. Jones. Hon. Sec,

Jim Murray told me that a large number of Allblacks supporters travelled with the team for their match against the Reds and the 'piccaninny in football togs', Mervyn Williams, led them onto the field in his Allblacks jersey. The only surviving accounts of the match are a newspaper report of the score from the *CFP* of 21 July 1923, and two oral history accounts:

I played football with 'em [Allblacks] for three or four years before I left 'em to play for the town team. Frankie Broughton was playing then, but I'd say his days was nearly finished. It was a good side too. We played all the top teams around here — Mandurama Reds...We went to play them and everybody laughed, thought it was a joke. But we came home victors. In them days they were a very big heavy side. I was the only little feller in the team. They were very big powerful fellers, the Murrays, the Bambletts, and the Carrol[l]s, the pack of forwards was that big, that anywhere they was a bit crooked on them, they used to call them the [G]laxo [a brand of baby food] babies. The Erambie Allblacks they called 'em[,] mostly all from Erambie. (Sam Kennedy in Read 1984b: 37)

They had a football team in Cowra, they called it the All Blacks. They went to a little town called Mandurama. The Mandurama Reds, they called them. They were supposed to be the best team in the west.

Then the Cowra blacks played them and beat them five to two. They couldn't believe it, it was a shock to all the Western District. They screened them, on the pictures they showed Cowra, the All Blacks beat them five to two. (Lachlan Ingram in Read 1984b: 37)

Although the detail of the score does not match the official record (the *CFP* on 21 July recorded an Allblacks' win by a score of 13 to 5), the meaning attached to the victory is clear in the accounts given by Ingram and Kennedy. Their accounts paint a picture of the sense of achievement the Erambie community got from beating such a highly regarded club as the Reds. I first heard about the Allblacks from the children of the players who skilfully told the story of the team's achievement. The Storyteller talked often about the Allblacks' win over the Reds. He probably heard it from his father who played in the team, or even his father-in-law who also played with the team. Jim told this story as part of another story about segregation at the local movie theatre. So much of my perception of the team and its players was invested in this victory that it was personally important not only that they beat the Reds, but that the Reds were worthy opponents. In fact, the story of the Allblacks' victory over the champion team is a continuing source of pride for many people within the Erambie community and is still told four generations after the match.

Sport and social inclusion

Geographic identification and rivalries between socio-economic groups can lead to an intense form of tribalism and a community can get a sense of itself through sport (Ruck 1993; Lansdown & Spillius 1990; Masters 2006). Bale states that sport 'is a world of hierarchy and territoriality' in his summary of the meaning attached to particular sporting teams (in Danielson 1997: 5). The above writers are among many who have examined the tribalism or loyalty to a certain team or social group that can be found in various forms of sport. At Erambie sport is one of the ways that people express a dearly held sense of community.

Wiradjuri people are traditionally territorial. This is illustrated in a warning given to Frank by his mother about leaving the safety of his own people: 'when you travel into a strange camp, my son, always pluck a gum leaf, carry it in your hand, walk in' (in Read 1984b: 11). Some years ago, I heard a Wiradjuri elder speak about the rivalries that were integral to the sporting festivals that were held within Wiradjuri country. He claimed that clan and tribe identification and pride were a part of the sporting festivals where the strongest athletes represented their group against others in athletic contests. The victories of the Erambie Allblacks are presented as examples of ability and worth of the men who represented the community. Tribalism remains a part of the Erambie Wiradjuri culture that can be seen in the storytelling of the Allblacks' victory over the Reds.

The way the Allblacks won their victory over the Mandurama Reds is described in the community's storytelling tradition and does not rely solely on perceptions of injustice and resistance. Rather, it is the skill of the athletes and the community they represent that is reinforced by their victory. It is probably true that some within the community viewed the victory as vindication against racism and oppression. However, this is not evident in the way this story was told to me. The dominant idea was that the victory over the Reds was affirmation that our athletes were worthy representatives of the community. The Storyteller often spoke about the athletic ability of his father and the Murray family, and the story of their victory over the champion Reds is told to reinforce this point. The victory also represents a continuation of the intense identification with a distinctively Wiradjuri identity.

Many of the community's social events were organised around the team. Dances were held to raise funds to cover expenses such as uniforms and to celebrate their victories. Sylvia remembered attending social events and football matches:

> I remember poor old Uncle Rueben Newton used to drive the bus. We went to Grenfell once when they played…They might have been raising money for the football team…I remember going to Reid's Flat once and they had a concert, I think they used to raise money for the football team to travel around because they paid for the bus, paid for the transport, for the bus and everything.

Shirley also recalled the link between the football team and social functions in her 1981 biography:

We used to have such fun. What I remember most about these days was the happiness and the laughing and the music. Uncle Lockey Ingram used to come on in and play the banjo-mandolin, and Uncle Sousy Ingram used to play the guitar or the violin, or someone would play music on gum-leaves, or blow combs. That was the sort of instruments we had in those days, not fancy instruments, but just anything that people could get a note out of, or a beat out of. They used to play all the old time waltzes, the Pride of Erin, Canadian Three Step, and sets, and we all used to dance, the youngest of us and the oldest. We all could dance in those days because you didn't have to throw your hip out of its socket and call that dancing. We used to have dancing for weddings and birthdays or when the Cowra footballers won the Mark's [sic] Cup. After the end of the football season, when the Erambie All-Blacks won the cup, there was dancing for three or four weeks. (in Smith & Sykes 1981: 12)

Senior men and women often talk about their fond memories of elders who organised dances. They talk about people rushing to get themselves ready to attend the dances.

How do oral history representations of the Allblacks' players compare to newspaper accounts of them? The newspapers had little that was good to say about the players as men. Instead, they stereotypically referred to them as morally inferior to white people. In contrast, within the community people speak about men who were the embodiment of heroism. They speak of men who organised family-friendly social functions. They speak of kind men who selflessly shared within the community no matter how meagre their own circumstances. They speak of forthright men who bravely confronted and defied government officials despite the constant threat of dire consequences such as the removal of children. They speak of men who taught children lessons about respecting elders and observing cultural practices during times of mourning. They speak about their fathers, uncles and brothers who represented the good of Wiradjuri culture.

Take the Storyteller's father as an example. When he played for the Allblacks, the *CFP* reported that he was responsible for a number of incidents of unfair play. In a 1923 match against the Pioneers it was reported that he 'played the man' with 'punching, rabbiting, illegal tackling and other rough play' (24 July 1923). In another match between the Allblacks and Pioneers, he was sent from the field twice. The newspaper claimed that he had used abusive language before 'vowing vengeance on all and sundry' (10 September 1929).

It is perhaps not surprising that the newspaper's depiction of a man's character is contrasted by the Storyteller's assessment of the man:

> My father had a wonderful streak in him. He took in older people from the place [the mission] and looked after them, you know. He looked after Uncle Sparrow until he died and made sure he was buried right. Daddy took him in and you know, looked after him, cos that's what they do, our people, you know, that's our culture. They talk about culture, that's what he did, took him in and they was mates, he was his *mudji* [friend]. Looked after him. Yeah, a wonderful man my father, well they all was, you know Uncle Buffalo, Uncle Major, Uncle Cutter and them, they was wonderful men. Men.

Whereas the newspapers painted a picture of men who represented an inferior group of people, the Erambie people talk about them as representative of a closely-knit and well-ordered Wiradjuri community.

The stories that heap praise on the men who played for the Allblacks are included as part of the wider yarning tradition. The men were often mentioned in passing during the long rambling yarns that I witnessed as a child. Through a lifetime of listening to praise of the men's abilities and character, I have developed a picture of them that contrasts with the way the newspapers represented them. I heard about men who had good community values and morals. They were men who were caring toward individuals and the community as a whole.

The training sessions the team held on the mission were also as much about community involvement as they were preparation for matches. According to Jim, the field on Erambie was the place to be in the evenings. Made from compacted dirt, the field was often illuminated using fire buckets and many community members were able to attend training sessions in the evenings. Jim's grandparents, Harry and Jane Murray, ensured everyone was included.

Community elders were the instigators of many of the sporting and social activities on the mission. For instance, the football team was formed by Harry Murray senior two years before an Aborigines Protection Board manager was appointed from outside the community. According to Sylvia, Harry and Jane Murray directed community elders to emphasise sport, music and dance to foster a sense of community. Sylvia remembered this sense of community as 'the most positive influence on [my] life'.

There are aspects of the inclusive way Erambie residents participated in football in the descriptions of Wiradjuri sporting culture at the point of early contact with white people. Descriptions of Wiradjuri games can be divided into two main categories. The first category of games is one that apparently develops survival skills among young people. My focus is on another category: the games that were mainly played for fun. Haagen summarised the European reaction to the inclusive nature of these fun games in the following way:

> Many of these writers, themselves the products of a Victorian ethos with its notions of propriety and decorum, found young and old often entangled in boisterous play — play that was designed not only to give expression to the abilities and skills of the players but to give expression to a community at leisure, full fed and finished for the moment with the tasks of subsistence. (Haagen 1994: 16)

Beveridge, writing in the journal *The Science of Man* in 1899, identified inclusion as an important element in the play of Murrumbidgee Wiradjuri clans. He found that their form of football and a skipping game included large numbers of people. A later account by Bowler in 1901 described how Lachlan River Wiradjuri played football with a ball made from 'opossum wool...as a group rather than in teams' (in Haagen 1994: 67). The Wiradjuri who were observed during early contact with white people had an active recreational life that included inclusive games.

Gordon, an Erambie elder, commented that the loss of 'traditions' was something that 'just happened, there was nothing spectacular about it, nothing sensational' (in Read 1984b: 15). To identify features of 'traditional' Wiradjuri games I have had to rely on descriptions provided by white observers. It is possible that traditional games evolved in a manner that was not sensational and therefore went largely unnoticed by young men such as Gordon who had grown up playing football on Erambie under the direction of elders. Rather than being seen as a significant event that would warrant inclusion in oral history, the evolution appears to have, in Gordon's words, 'just happened'. The European games apparently had benefits the traditional games did not have in a quickly changing society. The easier availability of leather footballs and the presence of teams to play may have contributed to the adoption of rugby league football. As a further example of this we can take the traditional Wiradjuri skipping game that was adapted for use on reserves. The intention of the game, 'to include large numbers of people' (Beveridge 1899: 49), remains a feature of this game even today. Skipping games using long lengths of synthetic rope were popular on Erambie during the 1970s, 1980s and 1990s when I was growing up there. These games were usually initiated by community elders and continued for hours at a time. It was not uncommon for all of the children on the mission and many of the adults to be playing at once. By using ropes made of synthetic material rather than the time-consuming traditional woven reeds, the Wiradjuri have been able to adapt and incorporate innovations when advances are beneficial.

The 'traditional' games of the Wiradjuri are linked to those played on the mission. The people of Harry Murray's generation were born during the 1870s so they may have learned from their parents the meanings attached to the traditional form of football played along the Lachlan River. Murray and his brother Sam played rugby for Cowra in the late 1890s and I have also documented his role as the leader of the Allblacks. Although I have no direct testimony that indicates that these elders intentionally transferred aspects of traditional football (such as an emphasis on inclusion) to rugby league, I do propose a logical link. Elders, led by Murray, initiated inclusive community events around football games. Attendance at many of the Allblacks games often included the entire camp, which indicates they were very successful in including the community in football games. There is persistence in the use of football as a community unifier that provides a link between the two forms of the game. As a result, it is not too big of a jump to conclude continuity of Wiradjuri sporting culture in this context. Community elders adapted traditional football to suit their modern needs. They did this while at the same time keeping important characteristics of the traditional game.

Some parts of 'traditional' games were retained and other elements evolved. Such retention of Indigenous cultures is not uncommon. To illustrate this point, if we take the 'traditional' culture from the Northern Territory, many of these groups use European cloth in their costumes, travel to ceremonies by motor car and even arrange ceremonies by mobile phone. Does this make the meaning of the dances any less authentic? Or, has the meaning of the ceremonies remained intact despite changes? Adapting some aspects of culture does not exclude Erambie's mission culture from being authentic. Also, the dominant view of what an Aborigine should be influences what is perceived as authentic. Just as the 'early travellers' were surprised at the amount of time spent playing games in Indigenous communities, it continues to surprise some that our culture involved more than boomerang making and corroborees. A change in approach to what is considered 'traditional' allows for the concept of continuity of Wiradjuri culture to be accepted in the context of sport.

Barnstorming Allblacks

From 1929 to 1944 the Allblacks travelled around the Western District playing invitational matches. In this period their reputation grew and the *CFP* referred to them as the 'famous Cowra All Blacks'. They made the transition from a club team to a sought-after travelling team. The representation of the Allblacks, and Aborigines in general, differs between newspapers. This can be attributed to the motivation of those offering the representations and resulted in a variety of Aboriginal identities being constructed through the Allblacks.

Following their 1925 victory over the Mandurama Reds, the Allblacks continued to play challenge matches against teams from Cowra and surrounding areas. They had victories against and losses to well-performing local teams. Their performances contributed to their growing reputation as football players. This led to them being given the distinction of an invitation to play the Bathurst District representative team in 1930 as the champion Reds had previously done. Prior to this match they were promoted in the Bathurst *National Advocate* as worthy opposition to the district team (6 June 1930). A photograph of the team was published in the *CFP* on a regular basis as the Allblacks were playing invitation matches throughout the western area.

Two features of the Allblacks' time as a sought-after 'invitational' team were the crowded match schedule and their willingness to play matches under less than

FIGURE 1

The Erambie Allblacks. Back row, left to right: Harry 'Major' Murray, Robert Carroll, Claude Murray, Alf 'Knocker' Williams, James 'Cutter' Bamblett, John Healand, Stanley Carroll, Ernest 'Buffalo' Whitty. Front row, left to right: Herbert 'Doolan' Murray, Alan Murray, Dave Perry, unknown, John Charles. (Author's collection)

FIGURE 2

The photograph of the 'famous Cowra All Blacks' that regularly appeared in the *Cowra Free Press*. This one was published on 6 May 1930.

FIGURE 3

Barnstorming Erambie Allblacks in 1929, prior to a match against Condobolin. Back row, left to right: Robert Carroll, possibly John Healand, Mr Downie (club secretary), Major Murray, John Charles; middle row, left to right: Frank Broughton, Frank Simpson, Doolan Murray, Paul Coe, Buffalo Whitty; front row, left to right: Stanley Carroll, Dave Perry, Claude Murray, Mervyn Williams (mascot), Jim Bamblett. (Courtesy Laurie Murray)

FIGURE 4

Erambie 'Baby Blacks' in 1937. Dickie McGuinness (seated with football) became a legendary figure in the local football scene. After the demise of the Allblacks, McGuinness, 'Ado' Carberry (standing, centre back row) and 'Bricky' Bamblett were joined by Jim and 'Viney' Murray (not pictured) in the Cowra Maher Cup team. These players made their names as football players with teams other than the Erambie Allblacks. (Author's collection)

FIGURE 5

The railway gates site. The houses on Erambie are in the background. The site is approximately 200 metres from the houses; however, it is directly outside the boundary line of the mission. (Photograph taken in 2004, author's collection)

FIGURE 6

An undated photograph of Wiradjuri leader Harry Murray senior, who was an accomplished athlete and leader of the Erambie Wiradjuri community until his death in 1938. Murray was a direct descendant of Wiradjuri leaders on the Lachlan River; however, his leadership of the Erambie community was linked to his own abilities and accomplishments more than to any hereditary right he may have possessed. (Courtesy June Murray)

FIGURE 7

Herbert 'Doolan' Murray. (Undated photograph, courtesy Margaret Murray)

FIGURE 9

Thirteen-year-old Jimmy Murray (in centre of picture) competing in 1936 in a 'Sheffield' or 'Gift' race at the Cowra Recreation Ground against adults, including Lachlan Ingram, one of the Erambie Allblacks (far right). Among the spectators are Jim's father and coach, Doolan Murray (fourth from left), and Robert Carroll senior (third from left). (Courtesy Jim Murray)

FIGURE 10

Jim Murray, the 'Black Prince', during his prime as an athlete at a Victorian race meeting. (Undated photograph, courtesy Jim Murray)

ideal circumstances. This may have affected their win–loss record but it did not damage their growing reputation. The team also started to include a musical 'pre game' show in the form of a gumleaf band from 1929 onwards to become a more complete entertainment package. Over time, they adapted their use of sport and music within the Erambie community to be a successful entertainment package for a general audience. This was similar to the 1868 Indigenous Australian touring cricket team that entertained audiences after matches using aspects of traditional culture (Mulvaney 1967; Mallett 2002). The link between sport and music was further strengthened as the newspapers reported that the gumleaf band started playing concerts around the district to raise money for the team.

In July and August of 1929 the Allblacks played invitation–charity matches in major Western District centres. The matches were against teams that were outside their usual competition. The newspaper reports on these matches varied in tone from mocking to respectful. The season began with challenge matches on successive days when the Allblacks travelled to Quandialla with a number of supporters. The *CFP* reported that the players and supporters were invited to a dance where their gumleaf band provided the entertainment after a 13–3 win by Erambie (20 May 1929). The *CFP* also reported that, the next day at the Cowra Recreation Ground, they played Mandurama in front of a 'very large crowd' (20 May 1929). This increase in frequency of matches brought with it an increase in newspaper articles. Within these articles there is some variation in the way the Allblacks (and Aborigines) are represented. In the *CFP*, for example, the team were often called the Cowra All Blacks or Cowra's Aboriginal FC or the Cowra All Backs as their reputation in the district grew. This is an obvious change from the earlier representations of the team when they were challenging the Cowra Pioneers.

The first of the five invitation matches (as opposed to challenge matches) that the team played in 1929 was against Junee in July. Junee's *Southern Cross* report on the match was 'contributed' to the *CFP*. The report contained the following description of the visit:

> The All Blacks, the much advertised Cowra team, arrived in Junee to-day (Wednesday) for the purpose of playing a match against the Juneeites. They came across by motor lorry, leaving Cowra at 5 o'clock, arriving in Junee just before 12…The gum-leaf band gave various selections round

the town before lunch and created much interest. After lunch they went to the ground to have a look round, and expressed appreciation of the manner in which they had been treated...Before commencement of the game the All Blacks gave a musical item, which was both clever and highly entertaining...The All Blacks 'cut' [the share of the entry fee money] of the gate was £35. (12 July 1929)

The remainder of the report contained a description of the play in the match that the Allblacks lost 31–22. Apart from noting the entertainment value of the Allblacks, the report does not contain stereotypical or derogatory representations of the team or Aborigines in general. It also describes the reputation the team was gaining and that they were now playing matches during the working week and not just on weekends.

The next game was at the invitation of the Condobolin Football Club less than two weeks later. In the report of this match, the issue of drawing the colour line again surfaced. This time, the Allblacks were not the target of exclusion. The *CFP* reported under the headline, 'Condo beat All Blacks', after a hard and friendly game:

Cowra and Condobolin hospitals benefit to the extent of nearly £11 each...after a great game, which was played in a splendid sporting spirit, victory rested with the home team by 9 points to 2...In connection with the above match we have received the following letter from...the Secretary to the Condobolin Club, and as requested by him we have handed over the cheque enclosed to President of the Cowra District Hospital. (23 July 1929)

The letter sent by the Condobolin club to the editor and published in the *CFP* gives some indication of how the Allblacks were able to negotiate issues of race and racism in sport (23 July 1929). It describes the interest in the game that presumably was connected to the race of the Allblacks team. The letter also indicates that the demand for the Allblacks as opponents was increasing to the point that they defied the normal practice by receiving payment for expenses:

We do not distribute gate tickets as a rule, although we did so to Cowra yesterday. It was a great game, there being 1200 people present

I am sure, counting children and the whole of the Condo. Mission camp, although charges are not made in their case. However, the Cowra boys are great sports, and made a great impression with the Condo. people...The Condobolin Club are greatly indebted to this team of sports, in assisting us to show the people of N.S.W. that the Condobolin Club do not draw any color [sic] line. (*CFP* 23 July 1929)

Another 1929 article was published under the headline: 'Challenge to Pioneers renewed' and reported that 'representatives of the All Blacks called at the "Free Press" to-day and stated that they think it is time the Pioneers either accept their challenge or refuse same'. The Allblacks representatives also expressed their preparedness 'to play any team' but preferably the Condobolin Boomerangs 'as it is thought the two coloured teams would prove a greater draw' (*CFP* 23 July 1929). The issue of white teams refusing to play black teams had come up again after a period of play between the Pioneers and Allblacks. There is no record of the Pioneers refusing to play the Allblacks during this period, although the article does mention that a challenge had not been answered. The Allblacks were apparently aware of the crowd-pulling ability of Aboriginality in district rugby league. Perhaps this is the reason the team had included the gumleaf band as part of their pre-match entertainment.

After the Pioneers — who, according to the *CFP* were 'reputed to have drawn the "colour line"' — accepted the Allblacks' challenge for a match 'on the most convenient date', the Erambie team continued travelling to invitational matches at other centres (30 July 1929). After their visit to Forbes, the Allblacks were represented in the *Western Sun* newspaper in a way that was consistent with stereotypical ideas about Aborigines:

Easily the best crowd seen at a rugby league game in Forbes this season, watched the local team defeat the Cowra All Blacks by 20 points to 14 at the cricket ground on Sunday...there was a roar of applause and cheers, leavened by the blare of motor horns, as the All Blacks (some blacker than others) took the field preceded by a diminutive picanniny in Guernsey, socks, tiny football boots, knee guards and all...S Carroll of the dark brigade, sustained an injury which necessitated a pow-pow in the centre of the field. After the medicine men had exorcised the 'debil-debil' the warrior resumed his place in the ranks and the battle proceeded...Alan Murray was only stopped from scoring because Ferguson stood as firm as the last of the Saxons in his path. (30 July 1929)

This is contrasted by a more respectful report on their next match in the *Grenfell Record* that relied much less on racial stereotypes:

> The visit of the Cowra All Blacks created a great deal of interest, and there was a large crowd present on Sunday to witness the match. The first quarter of an hour was sensational, as the Blacks, by their wonderful handling of the ball, put it well and truly over the locals who were beaten by the speed of the visitors...The game was one of the best witnessed here this season, and the visitors made themselves very popular by their fine game and good sportsmanship. The mascot of the team — a tiny picanniny — dressed in football togs, led them on to the field. During the half time interval the All Blacks entertained those present with some very fine music, the gum-leaf artist producing some very fine music. (9 August 1929)

In yet another match report, this time from the *Young Daily Witness*, the Allblacks were again represented in a stereotypically racist way. The article included the headline, 'Stage football circus':

> By far the biggest crowd of the season gathered at the cricket ground on Sunday to see the Cowra aboriginal team, the 'All Blacks' play Young... The abos were a hefty lot and trotted out to the accompaniment of much 'tooting' and applause...The statement that the All Blacks played barefooted was not borne out as they were all in proper rig-out, much better even than the Young side...the All Blacks tackled well and handled well, but only about three of them knew anything about football. The crowd was tickled to death at the antics of the visitors who were full of jokes. Every time they tackled a man they picked him up and apologised, 'sorry cobber'...Once, Young broke quickly from a scrum and...scored 'that's no plurry good,' said one of the darkies, 'we weren't ready dat time.'...The gate totalled £30, but should have been much more, many passing through the gate and refusing to pay. This was meanness of the worst type and even the darkies commented on

it. 'Too many plurry dead-eds,' said one of them, disgustedly. They were getting half the gate money. (23 August 1929)

This type of description appears to be linked to the predetermined stereotype of Aborigines. This can be seen in the expectation that the Allblacks would play barefoot. In addition, claiming that most of the Allblacks knew nothing about football was linked to stereotypes rather than the team's previous achievements.

When the Allblacks did renew their rivalry with the Cowra Pioneers the placement of the reports is as interesting as the language used in them. For example, when the Allblacks defeated the Pioneers in front of a 'large attendance', the *CFP* reported the match as being 'chiefly remarkable for its hard tackling and lack of brilliance'. Other than commenting on the 'unmistakable signs of glee' that the 'Allblacks and their supporters' exhibited at the result, no description of the play is given in the brief article (27 August 1929). Contrast this with the large front-page article of 10 September, which included the headline 'Pioneers turn tables on All Blacks' and incorporated a photograph of the defeated Allblacks team. It detailed the good play of the Pioneers along with the 'cries of derision' directed at the referee from the 'Allblacks barrackers, of whom there were a considerable number' (10 September 1929).

Another example of variation in the way the Allblacks were represented can be seen in a 1933 report on their Gleeson Cup-winning match against Wattamondara. The report was contributed by Major Murray who was excluded from playing with the team when he played for Cowra in the senior competition. Murray's report, published in the *CFP*, is unique in that it gives some insight into how the players saw themselves and their supporters:

> The bell sounds and Flannery and his hefty giants take the field, soon followed by E Whitty [Allblacks] and his team of stalwarts… Soon the boys [are] hard at it…playing like Trojans the 'All Blacks' are soon rewarded, a great try being scored by Eric Onus, after nearly the whole team had handled the 'pigskin'. This movement was a real gem and would have done credit to any class of football…The spectators are now at concert pitch and all efforts to keep them off the line are useless. The 'All Blacks' are still playing great football

and [Wattamondara] seem to be wilting under the strain. Men are dropped, kicked and punched, yet they rise again and dive in hard and solid...The 'All Blacks' handling is now a pleasure to watch...The Cup being handed over to the victors a good days sport is brought to a close. (29 June 1933)

Murray's match report reversed the usual roles of representations of the Allblacks. In his report the Aborigines were the heroes who 'rise again' against the physical presence of the 'hefty' white opposition and rouse their supporters to 'concert pitch'. In this case the emphasis was placed on the moral character of the Allblacks as they represented their community against a physical other in a way that they could be proud of. Murray gave a detailed description of the free-flowing, skilful style of play that their supporters appreciated. Not even after their impressive victory over the Reds did the *CFP* describe the Allblacks as heroes. Within all of the variation in the way the team was represented in newspaper reports, they were never the heroic until this report.

Hamilton's 1981 concept of the 'illusory correlation' seems to have operated to associate Aborigines with a distinctive type of behaviour in the newspaper reports. Hamilton argued in 1989 that when a minority is not seen much and one of them is seen performing a distinctive act they, as a group, can be associated with that act (Hamilton & Sherman 1989: 59–82). The way the *CFP* described Aborigines associated them with distinctive acts. A *Bulletin* cartoon reprinted in the *CFP* illustrates this point. It links Aborigines with the distinctively negative act of begging, while depicting an Aborigine as the comically scruffy Jacky-Jacky character typically bothering a white man (29 August 1930). The Jacky-Jacky character 'tortures' the English language (Leab 1975: 8). This commonly held stereotype of the time was quickly and effectively depicted in the cartoon. The Jacky-Jacky character was used to represent the Allblacks and associated them with these stereotypical ideas about Aborigines.

Studying the language of stereotyping is worthwhile because language is a medium of constructing knowledge as well as of communicating it (Hinton 2000). The media play an important role in forming and communicating these social representations (Hinton 2000). Some district newspapers used specific language to construct a negative representation of the Allblacks and the Aborigines. This means that the Allblacks played a role in creating knowledge about Aborigines. Their supposed inability to master the English language was emphasised by people who wished to reinforce the idea that Aborigines are inferior to white people. At this point it may be useful to repeat the following quote from Frantz Fanon about representations of colonised people:

> I ascribe a basic importance to the phenomenon of language…Every colonised people finds itself face to face with the language of the civilising nation; that is, with the culture of the mother country. The colonised is elevated above his jungle status in proportion to his adoption of the mother country's cultural standards. (Fanon 1952/1970: 14)

Although we might draw inferences from the language used to represent Aborigines, it should be remembered that language has context-dependent meaning. In the context of colonisation the stereotypical representation of the way black races speak is considered evidence of inferiority (Leab 1975). Pickering has termed this 'nigger vernacular' and says it is used to reinforce the inferior position of blacks. The language reported to be used by Aborigines should be termed 'Jacky vernacular' because of its relationship to the caricature that suggests inferiority (Pickering 2001: 121). Marqusee writes that Fanon and others who have examined the process of colonisation studied the psychology of the colonised in their writing (1999). Marqusee makes an important point about viewing the responses of colonised peoples in the context of their situation. However, the representations of colonised peoples also reveal much about the coloniser. For example, the representations of the Allblacks expose a need by some white people to manage the identity of Aborigines.

The *CFP* published a joke in 1924 about the 'Jacky' character that suggested Aborigines were lazy and untrustworthy (12 February 1924). In 1927, a district newspaper reprinted a *Bulletin* cartoon that associated the Jacky language to an unidentified black footballer, presumably the Jacky character. The player, comically trapped under an obese referee, complains, 'by korry, worst referee I ever played under'. The cartoon was published on 29 June 1927 when the Allblacks were regularly invited to play Western District teams.

Although a number of inferences may be drawn from this cartoon, it seems fair to suggest a link between the most identifiable Indigenous footballers of the district and the stereotypical intention of the cartoon. A further example of this connection being made between the Allblacks and the Jacky vernacular can be seen in the reports of some of their matches. The *Young Daily Witness* characterised the Allblacks as the comical Jacky-Jacky when they were reported to be 'full of jokes' and using Jacky vernacular such as 'that's no plurry good' and 'we weren't ready dat time' (23 August 1929). The similarities in a report from Forbes' *Western Sun* offer some possible insights into the motivation for representing the Allblacks in this way. In this case the Jacky character of the 'dark brigade' was contrasted with the local team of steadfast 'Saxons' (30 July 1929). Pickering builds on the work of Said and Fanon among others who have associated stereotyping with the process of forming an identity against an 'other' (2001). In this case it seems that the stereotyped representation of the Allblacks was used to create an 'other' that was integral in creating the identity of the home team. This identity was created not just in the context of the games but also in the midst of calls for a prosperous white Australia.

No more Allblacks

In spite of the onset of the Great Depression, it appeared as though the Allblacks could look forward to a bright future. They had the Gleeson and Eandly Challenge cups in their possession, and their junior team, the 'Baby Blacks' were producing some 'elusive' and talented players, a point made regularly in the *CFP*'s football reports. In 1938 the Allblacks played in their first graded matches as part of a Cowra district competition. However, this decade would also see dramatic changes within the Erambie community as well as to the structure of rugby league in the district. Even with the Allblacks' growing fame, these changes were influential factors in bringing the successful run of this unique football team to an end.

The Allblacks were an ageing team. Many of the players who had built its reputation were in their thirties, and some were in their late forties. In many cases the long careers of the players was probably a necessity due to the small population of the community. The Storyteller said that his father and Cutter Bamblett, for instance, were in their mid-thirties when they played their first games in 1922. The star of the team, Major Murray, continued to play until 1941 when he was 41 years of age. The team continued to play despite the difficulties in maintaining player numbers for the still-small community. This could indicate that they were aware of the important role the team played in the Erambie community. However, those players could not continue indefinitely and the task of organising a team to play matches appears to have increased in difficulty.

Perhaps the most significant change to the community came after the deaths of the two recognised community leaders, Jane Murray on 22 August 1937 and Harry Murray senior on 2 December 1938. The death of these two leaders, who were instrumental in organising the team, contributed greatly to the team's demise. The loss of Harry and Jane Murray must have been devastating for a community that had relied on their leadership since its inception. For the next generation of leaders on Erambie, the use of football in community socialising appears to have changed slightly as the game itself progressed to a new format.

Another important change for the Allblacks' future was the formation of group competitions which changed rugby league in the Western District dramatically. The move away from the challenge system that allowed players some freedom to move between teams to the weekly competition matches forced them to play with one team per season. This also put an end to many old rivalries such as the Allblacks and Pioneers. The Allblacks' traditional rivals, the Pioneers, became part of a unified Cowra team that joined the Group Nine Competition. The Pioneers played in the prestigious Maher Cup competition while the Allblacks were demoted to a reserve grade competition.

Still, in 1938 the Allblacks did play in a regular competition for the first time. The *Lachlan Leader* (hereafter *Leader*), which had evolved from the *CFP*, reported that a Cowra district reserve grade competition was formed at the request of Cowra businessman Dan Gleeson, who had been sponsoring a challenge cup trophy for district teams (2 June 1938). Subsequently, the Gleeson Challenge Cup, which the Allblacks had held for two years, was formed into a regular reserve grade competition. The restrictions placed on player movements and the relegation of the Allblacks to a reserve grade competition made it hard for them to retain players. The Cowra team could offer Erambie's new generation of players better opportunities to play top-class competition. Nevertheless, the Allblacks' management did not simply accept the changes to their status and they protested against the loss of their players. This can be seen in a *Leader* article headlined: 'All Blacks aggrieved', that described a letter the team sent to the Cowra Rugby League to express their resentment at losing rising star Jim Murray, son of the Allblacks' first captain, Doolan, to the Cowra Maher Cup (9 June 1938).

The Allblacks continued to challenge first grade teams while they were playing in the reserve grade competition. An advertisement for one such match includes a reserve grade fixture as the 'early game'. This may be a good indication of the Allblacks seeing themselves as a main-attraction team rather than a reserve grade or support team. Despite losing players and being demoted, the team's reputation allowed them to defy the usual practice of the time and continue to play first grade teams. The advertisement encouraged readers to 'See the Nippy All Blacks in Action!' against Blayney (*Leader* 2 June 1938).

In addition to losing players to other rugby league teams, the Allblacks faced a challenge from Australian rules football, recently introduced to the Cowra area. Two men from Victorian Aboriginal reserves lived on Erambie for a time and they were possibly responsible for encouraging residents to try Australian rules football. Although the new code of football never seriously challenged rugby league in the long term, in 1940 many of the Allblacks' players were playing both codes. As had been the case in rugby league, Erambie footballers started playing with Cowra teams but soon sought their own team. The 'Aussie Rules' reporter, 'Punt', described the 1940 introduction of Erambie players to the new game in the *Leader*:

> The Erambie contingent comprised: Major Murray — he's still got plenty of dash. Claude Atkinson — a player of class if he fulfils the promise shown. Alex Briggs — an 'old hand' at the game who'll be an asset to the Erambie team. Ray and Merv. Williams — two nippy lads. Harold Carberry and Viney Murray — rugby stars who'll star also at the national code. Dick McGuinness and A. Bamblett — who, like their fellow Erambie players, should take to the game like ducks to water. It will not be long before Erambie issues a challenge to Cowra to a game. (9 May 1940)

Another player not mentioned in the article, Jim Murray (who, the *Leader* reported, the Allblacks were already fighting other rugby league clubs to keep), would show enough promise to be offered a contract of 8 pounds per week to play with the South Melbourne Club (28 March 1940). Jim told me that he eventually played for the St Kilda club in the Victorian Football League before starting a long and successful career in a Victorian regional competition. The Allblacks were facing challenges from a number of areas when it came to retaining their talented players.

During this period the team was forced to enlist supporters from the crowd, who on occasion played in bare feet, to form a team. This is in contrast to the 1920s when the team played with a set group of players who turned out for most matches 'in better rig out' than their opponents. Changes that led to the Allblacks not playing were gradual and were related to changes in the sport and within the community itself. However, after the collapse of the regular reserve grade competition they simply stopped playing.

In August 1940 the Allblacks played their last reported match against a team from Cowra called Railway. The next generation of Allblacks were then described in the *Leader* in similar terms to their fathers and uncles, with an emphasis on their athletic ability:

> In one of the fastest and most open games seen on the Cowra recreation ground for some time, All Blacks yesterday defeated Cowra Railway combination by 23 points to six. All Blacks completely outplayed Railway, mainly due to their superior speed and better combination… Throughout, it was a particularly fast and open game. Some brilliant passing rushes were staged by the All Blacks and their combination was superb. The Murray brothers, Carberry and McGuinness were [the] outstanding players of their side. (3 August 1941)

Up until the end, the Allblacks team remained a focal point for the community at Erambie. On 7 July 1941 the *Leader* reported on their 'successful dance in the mission school hall to raise money for the football club'. Even though there were references to the team, there is no record of them playing matches in the Western District after the August 1940 encounter with the Railway team.

The final reference to the 'Famous Allblacks' in a Cowra newspaper was when the *Leader* referred to their challenge to the Cowra Maher Cup team (18 August 1941). Challenging such a well-performing team indicated belief in their own ability. The article also noted that the Allblacks were thinking of contesting matches in the Maher Cup the following year. Although the match did not eventuate, the report indicated that the 'undefeated All Blacks' had challenged the Cowra representative team. Therefore, the 'Famous Erambie Allblacks' ended as they had started, by asserting their ability and challenging Cowra's best team.

The Erambie Allblacks re-emerged with the introduction of Koori rugby league carnivals in the late 1970s. Gone were the gold and maroon team colours, replaced with a new standard of Koori identity: the 1981 Erambie Allblacks bore the colours of the Koori flag. The colours represented a more developed unity and political awareness among Aborigines. The 1979 version of the team was organised by Agnes Coe whose husband Les Coe was the grandson of Harry and Jane Murray, the original organisers of the team. The Coe family were players in the human rights activism of the 1970s. Paul Coe, a prominent player in the human rights movement, was among the organisers of the reformed Erambie Allblacks. Still, it does not follow that the rebirth of the team was only a reaction to anything that happened in the mainstream community. The Allblacks reformed to compete in a Koori rugby league carnival. In fact, the Erambie Allblacks created their own knockout competition. Attempts to rejoin old rivals in local competitions in 1987, 2004 and 2005 were rejected.

Today, the Erambie Allblacks play in annual Koori rugby league carnivals. One feature of the current Allblacks team is the community involvement it continues to generate. Erambie football has never been limited to young males but inclusive of the entire community. In this regard the team has continued to be important to the way that the community organises itself socially and culturally.

The stereotypical representations of the original Allblacks are examples of a discourse of deficit resulting from social breakdown and discontinuity of colonised cultures. As Fanon might have predicted, the Allblacks team became a signifier of two main identities. The first came from outside of the Erambie community where the enduring identity of an inferior 'other' unable to reach white people's standards of behaviour dominated the narrative. The vast majority of district newspapers described the Allblacks in a way that was in line with racial thinking of the time. They were represented as an inferior remnant of a dying race. This suggests that the newspapers were not willing to depart from the dominant racial theories. Instead, they described the Allblacks in a way that reinforced the idea of racial differences. When the reputation of the Murray family contradicted the theories of innate inferiority, they were separated from their kin on the mission. This can be seen in the 1923 *CFP* description of the Allblacks, with the exception of the Murrays, as unfair and dirty players. The Murray family was 'explained' in terms of racial thought in line with ideas about race being a floating signifier (Hall 1997) and concepts of expectation relating to 'place' (Douglas 1966/2002).

From an alternative perspective, within the Erambie community the football team was seen as an example of how Wiradjuri culture has persisted. It never seemed to occur to those who wrote about the Allblacks that the team could be representative of positive Wiradjuri cultural and social values. However, this is how the people of Erambie represent the players individually and the team collectively. This comes through in the storytelling about the team.

The way the Allblacks were represented helped to produce particular ways of knowing Aborigines. Two significant identities were placed on the Aborigines through the team. One comes from the white community and is greatly influenced by stereotypes of Aborigines. The other identity comes from within the Erambie community itself and is linked to a desire to maintain a connection with pre-contact Wiradjuri culture.

Chapter 4

Fighting at the gates

> They [the managers] didn't understand the culture of our people. They didn't understand what the little biff or whatever was about. See, maybe I can align it to American states where they used to call it a duel where you go there with your one shot gun to protect your honour. You go out and take twenty paces, turn around and shoot each other. So I can sort of align our culture with that. But brother, they [white people] just didn't understand.
> (Lachlan)

Bare-knuckle fights are among the most common shared community events on Erambie Mission. These fights are important to Erambie people because they are an effective way to manage disputes. The fights also connect generations to Wiradjuri culture. There are contrasts in the ways the practice of fighting within the Erambie community was and is represented. The government-appointed managers' descriptions of fights on Erambie contributed greatly to the way fights were known outside the community. The interest shown by researchers since the 1960s in contemporary mission life placed the fights into a wider context and introduced theoretical explanations. These studies presented the first accounts of fighting that included voices from within the community and, in so doing, introduced a different way of understanding them.

Old ways and new

Early European observers of Kooris described fights between individuals and groups of warriors that were highly ritualised and controlled. Prolonged warfare between groups was uncommon (Reed 1969). In 1815 Governor Macquarie reported to his superiors in London that the Wiradjuri of the Bathurst area were 'by no means savage or warlike' (in Folster 1998: 47). In another instance, a record was made of a ritualised fight between two clan leaders from the Tumut area in 1832 (Howitt 1996; Flood 1980). While the Wiradjuri were not recorded as being war-like, at least in their dealings with white settlers, they were known to use ritualised fighting to settle disputes.

Drawing on first-hand accounts, Martin writes that the fighting customs of the clans of the upper Murrumbidgee region were 'highly ritualised ways of dealing with problems common to all societies' (1978: 85). He uses written accounts as examples of ritualised fighting still occurring in 1863. He describes one fight in the Queanbeyan district from 1863:

> After a quarter of a century of white settlement, a mixture of traditions was emerging, and the fight was conducted like a boxing match, with… Jimmy Taylor as referee. A venue was fixed near one of the Tuggeranong homesteads, and a large white crowd gathered to see the fun. To their amused disappointment, although the two men smashed at each other's shields with their nullas, and made a great deal of noise, only one glancing blow was struck in seven rounds. (in Martin 1978: 86)

Although the exact source is not identified, this account appears to have come from a European who witnessed the event. It suggests that elements of boxing were introduced to traditional dispute management techniques gradually over a twenty-five-year period. The incorporation of European materials and culture had already been going on for some time. However, archaeologist Jim Kelton found evidence of Wiradjuri people, such as those at Wellington, resisting attempts to completely dissociate them from their culture as far back as the 1830s:

> [B]y the late 1830s, a tug-of-war was occurring between Christian missionaries Watson and Gunther and the Wiradjuri elders, mainly over the continuation of initiation and the 'rites of passage' of uninitiated young boys. (1997: 17)

Wiradjuri people considered camps such as Erambie as places where assimilation could be resisted (Kelton 1997). Attempts to convert Wiradjuri people to Christianity 'led to irreparable damage to black–white relations'

(Kelton 1997). Wiradjuri elders entered into the 'mission era' with a desire to maintain valued cultural practices while incorporating aspects of European cultures that enhanced these practices.

In 1926, one of the first white people to settle in Wiradjuri country, Sarah Musgrave, described fights between local clans that took place in the area close to Erambie as highly organised.

> The method of fighting was for the armies to face one another at a short distance and to throw spears and boomerangs until the battle was declared closed. Each side would then bury its dead, after which the tribes would return to their respective camping grounds. (Musgrave 1926: 15–16)

Fighting with a clenched fist is not 'as natural and spontaneous an activity as might be thought', according to Corris who claimed that fighting with weapons was the norm in human combat (1979: 4). Boxing evolved as a sport in ancient Greece and Rome then went into a decline before it re-emerged in Britain in the eighteenth century (Bachelor 1948). It was introduced to Australia via ties with Britain before white settlers came into Wiradjuri country, and they probably introduced the sport through the gold mining camps that sprung up in the area (Marriott 1988). Pugilism was introduced to Australia with the First Fleet even though the first recorded prize fight in Australia was not until 1814. The Australian population was made up of a 'preponderance of fighting classes' with established fighters transported during their fighting prime, making Australia a place where pugilism could thrive (Brailsford 1988: 141). Boxing came to the Western District through the goldfields, which were an early nursery for the sport (Corris 1979). When the first reports of boxing appeared in the *Cowra Free Press* (*CFP*) in 1906, Jimmy Sharman was working in Cowra's sheep industry — he went on to become an institution in Australian boxing due to his involvement in the travelling tent shows.

Managing identity

By the time the Aborigines Protection Board managers arrived at Erambie, the practice of using boxing in dispute management was established. The appointment of mission managers marked the beginning of the period in which the newspapers began reporting on fighting at Erambie. While early settlers' accounts were largely descriptive, the managers produced very negative representations of Wiradjuri fighting. The managers' representations of the fighting from 1924 until 1955 greatly influenced the responses of government officials. These responses generally involved attempts to control the practice, which in turn led to reaction from within the community.

The managers' accounts of the fights were regularly recorded in official reports to their superiors as well as periodically appearing in local newspaper articles. It was largely due to the managers that fighting on the mission was regarded as a problem. Their intervention usually resulted in court appearances and prosecutions, which were subsequently reported in newspapers. Both the courts and the newspaper articles accepted the managers' evidence, which suggests that their points of view were often considered accurate. In the absence of Wiradjuri voices, the managers' interpretations of the fighting were to this point the only ones on record.

One manager, J Foster (described by Sylvia as 'the best of a bad lot'), was particularly influential in representing Erambie fighting practices to non-Indigenous people. He spent thirty years in the employment of the Board, including ten as the manager of Erambie, and during this time he was considered an expert on Aborigines. His status as an expert probably added weight to his interpretations of the fights on the mission.

Foster's opinions of the fighting within the Erambie community do not seem to have been challenged outside the community. His opinions seem to have been influential in the representations of the fighting and the people who participated in it. He informed the people of Cowra about what he claimed was negative behaviour of Kooris through newspaper articles, and also, via his reports to the Board, gave the managers who followed him at Erambie notice of what to expect.

Between 1932 and 1940 Foster repeatedly called the police and had residents charged with criminal offences when he discovered them fighting on the mission. This in turn led to court action, which was then reported by the newspapers. These reports invariably included headlines that focused on the race of those involved and described the fights as unacceptably negative behaviour. For example, on 9 January 1939 an article in the *Lachlan Leader* (hereafter *Leader*), headlined 'Coloured men charged', described how two Erambie residents had 'roused the neighbourhood' with their fighting. This is contrasted by another report on the same page that briefly outlined charges against non-Indigenous men involved in a fight without referring to their racial background.

Foster gave evidence in a number of court cases that resulted from fights on Erambie. His descriptions, given in evidence, were included in the newspaper reports of these events. On 8 April 1932, two *CFP* articles appeared under the headlines: 'Thought it was a corroboree: Disturbance at Erambie Mission', and 'Fight at mission station: two men fined for disorderly conduct'. Foster is reported as giving evidence that two men 'fought like tigers' and that 'there was great danger of a riot being caused'. Following an earlier fight, the *CFP* reported that Foster testified that he had called the police even though Erambie elder Harry Murray warned him not to intervene in a community matter which was under his control (5 January 1932). The intrusions of the manager contributed to the use of the railway gates site, which was outside the mission boundary.

The managers lived in a fenced-off compound at the edge of the mission. However, they regularly came onto the mission to conduct inspections of houses and to enforce Board rules. When they discovered fighting on the mission they attempted to stop it, which usually meant police intervention that resulted in arrests and prosecution for those involved in the fights. When the fighters attended court the evidence of the manager invariably led to convictions, and fines and gaol terms were issued. According to the *CFP*, one magistrate stated that he intended to treat two Erambie men leniently at the suggestion of the manager (5 February 1932). Both men were fined. On another occasion, the *Leader* reported that an Erambie man was fined and threatened with gaol when 'proceeded against' by Foster (19 January 1939). While the managers probably did not witness all the fights on the mission, their daily and monthly reports, along with the involvement of the police, did mean that the fights became public knowledge. Two *CFP* articles, from 5 February 1932 headlined: 'Fight at mission station', and 8 April 1932 headlined: 'Thought it was a corroboree', gave the manager's versions of fights that occurred on the mission. The articles' headlines also used language that reinforced Foster's view of the fights as 'disorderly' behaviour.

In addition to his testimony in court cases and official reports, Foster gave a description of the people of Erambie in an address to the Cowra Teachers' Association in 1934. A reporter from the *CFP* attended, and published a report of the address on 16 August 1934. In his speech, Foster is reported as making a distinction between 'their black predecessors and mission residents', and stated: 'we people of today know little of the better class of black and judge the race upon the class we do know.'[1] He continued, 'it must be remembered that the Aborigines are a child like race...because of their natural love of freedom they resent authority'. Taken together, Foster's documented opinions on Aborigines were generally negative. The public address he gave was not a regular occurrence but its inclusion in the local newspaper did ensure it reached a wider audience within the town than just those who attended the meeting. There is no record of the teachers, or any other person from the town, objecting to his statements.

With the exception of Foster's ten-year appointment, Erambie had a regular turnover of managers, and they all represented fighting as a problem and attempted to put a stop to it. In 1953, for example, men from each of the families living at Erambie were charged with fighting and had to attend court. The police were repeatedly called in to prevent continued 'brawling'. The manager's description of the fights as a problem came twenty-nine years after outsiders first recorded their impression of fights on the mission. This level and duration of involvement indicates that at least some people in the community did not share the desire to have the fights stopped.

The managers considered fighting a serious problem and they insisted on enforcing Aborigines Welfare Board rules to stop it. Eight men were prosecuted for 'drinking and fighting' on the reserve during September 1954 alone. Repeat offenders were fined for fighting on the mission. The Board responded to continued prosecutions for fighting with threats of expulsion. Mavis remembered two relatives who were threatened with expulsion in 1954 because the manager accused them of 'causing a lot of trouble'. Men who were repeatedly involved in fights were expelled from Erambie. Mavis read me a letter sent to her uncle in 1954 that stated, 'you have been repeatedly warned by the manager about your conduct but apparently take no notice'. The idea that the people 'took no notice' may not have been completely accurate because the people of Erambie did move the fighting area off the reserve sometime after 1924 in response to the manager's actions. However, despite the residents' efforts to avoid the intrusion of outsiders, in July 1954 alone seven men from the reserve were charged with fighting. They appeared in court and in local newspaper reports. They did, however, 'take no notice' of the outsiders' opinion that fighting should be stopped, and the ritualised practice of fighting to settle disputes continued through the era of Board management — and continues today, though no longer at the railway gates. In the stories that I have been told about the reactions of the Board to fights, the expulsion orders are worn as badges of honour. Similarly, there is great pride within the community that outsiders were not successful in their attempts to stop the fighting on the mission.

The fights took place in a Wiradjuri community that was undergoing many changes. Colonisation led to the formation of larger Wiradjuri communities such as Erambie. So, even though traditional kin relationships remained, the changes brought a much larger group of people together in a very small space. Along with the introduction of alcohol, this has undoubtedly increased the incidences of fighting. However, although the changes may have increased the number of instances when the fights were needed, the traditional use and method of the fights appears to be largely intact. Of course, the method of ritualised fighting did include fist fights which took the form of boxing. Still, the use of fighting to settle disputes remained constant through the mission era.

Without any contrary points of view, the opinions of the managers were apparently accepted by Board officials, police, and court officials, and presented to the general public by the local newspapers. This absence of Wiradjuri voices from documentary sources continued until researchers started to give people from Erambie an opportunity to explain how we view the practice of settling disputes with violence.

Why do they fight?

Beginning in the 1960s, non-Indigenous researchers developed an interest in examining Erambie's contemporary Wiradjuri culture. The following account of a fight story, told to Macdonald by two sisters, became the first published testimony on the fights from within the community. Notice the similarity between this 1991 description of the way the fights were conducted and the earlier 1926 description of Wiradjuri fighting from Musgrave. In particular, notice the similarity in the way the clans faced each other before the battle and returned to their homes when the battle was declared closed:

> Up at the gates, that's where they had the fighting ring — and underneath the railway bridge…They'd have a fight, but the next morning, they'd go up to the bridge or up to the gates and they'd fight it out: I'll see you in the morning. Yes…called them out the next morning…pull them out up there…all the [members of one family] on one side and all the [members of another family] on this side. 'Now!' he said, 'they're gonna have fightin. I don't want no barrackin,' [the referee] said. 'Now, no interference!' he [the referee] said. 'I'm the referee — no-one else gets in'…And [a woman from the mission], that when [she] started then: 'Go on…give it to him,' and he [the referee] said, '… that'll do now.' It woulda end up in a big brawl, see. Anyhow, two or three rounds and down went [one of the fighters] 'Oh! No more!' That was it then…they left it like that. 'No more then,' someone said. (in Macdonald 1991: 179)

The fights were of value to the community because they were legitimate tools for social interaction. In addition, the fights had value to the storytelling tradition within the community. The fights at the railway gates performed a number of functions within the community. There was, and continues to be, value to 'proper fights' in that they brought community division to a 'formal end' (Macdonald 1986: 190). Macdonald represented the fights overall as valuable and honourable, and explained them in part by aligning them with duels of honour. This change in approach to representing the fights came from the testimony offered by community members.

The story Macdonald was told differs from those I had been told in the amount of attention paid to the result of the fight. A feature of the fight stories I have been told is the lack of emphasis or outright omission of the result. This is, I believe, linked to the intended use of the stories to instil the value of settling disputes the 'proper way'. The results were also undoubtedly excluded so as not to cause embarrassment to any family. In a lifetime of listening to the stories about the fights at the gates I can recall only two occasions where the result of a fight was mentioned. On one occasion the result was only mentioned as part of the message that the winner ended the fight when they realised their opponent had 'had enough'. To continually tell of a fighter losing would cause resentment from the person, or their family, and probably result in further fighting. Therefore, just as the elders did not allow observers to be involved in barracking during fights, storytellers generally do not belittle anyone by focusing on the result of fights. I can only speculate that the two sisters who told Macdonald this story did not expect the story to become known within the Erambie community. This would have been a reasonable assumption on their part, considering that academic research was rarely returned to the people. Telling the result could have also been brought about by the influence of the researcher's questions. Whatever the reason, including results is not a feature of fight stories as I know them.

Macdonald theorised about how fighting could and should be viewed. She observed: '[n]o particular concern evinced about the fact a fight was taking place — although there was concern that it should be a fair fight' (1986: 170). From this starting point she examined why fighting was a 'normal' part of everyday life. Ironically, Macdonald wrote that she was 'initially struck' by 'the way in which people spoke about' the fights (1986: 170). In an effort to understand the fights her approach was to make comparisons between descriptions from early settlers who witnessed fights and the fights she had witnessed within the Erambie mission community. From this, she suggested that a link between or persistence of important elements of this traditional cultural practice was present and that differences in the value systems by which the fights were defined could be identified. She also noted that Erambie residents were aware of these differences and that it appeared to outsiders that the fights were evidence of a loss of traditional social patterns (Macdonald 1986).

Until researchers took an interest in contemporary mission culture and oral histories were collected, the accounts and representations of the managers were the only ones available outside the community. This meant that the public could learn about 'riotous behaviour' and 'brawling' on the mission rather than honourable fights used to settle disputes. This in turn led to the fights, which were usually reported with the caste of participants included, being linked to a loss of culture and authenticity. Therefore, each instance of fighting on the mission possibly contributed to an identity of the mission Aborigines as inauthentic.

In more recent academic representations, terms such as 'persistence' and 'continuity' (of culture) replaced managers' descriptions of 'brawling' and 'riots' as the defining terms. The use of the former terms suggests a link between initial descriptions of Wiradjuri and contemporary fighting practices on Erambie. The link focuses on persistence in the descriptions of fights, which would indicate a continuity of 'traditional culture' rather than the more accepted model of loss. Macdonald's work represents a shift in the type of language used to represent the fights.

Fights within some contemporary Indigenous communities have been described as highly ritualised and open displays of violence within the confines of normal daily life. Keating (1994) and McKnight (1986) have both described the way fights can erupt within Indigenous communities. McKnight described how people who were generally 'polite, friendly, warm-hearted and good humoured' suddenly transformed into 'aggressive, swearing and dangerous antagonists' (1986: 136). In their studies the fights are generally presented as a way of maintaining social order and personal and family honour.

However, McKnight observed that the use of weapons still existed in an Indigenous community in the 1960s and 1970s, which suggests some communities retained the more dangerous form of fighting (1986). The differences between the Queensland Indigenous community McKnight described and Erambie could shed light on why Erambie residents used the less dangerous way to fight. Unlike some mission and reserve communities, Erambie was built around long-established kin relationships, whereas the 'supercamp' McKnight described brought together unrelated groups of people who had had a previous violent relationship, and the level of violence remained high in their fights. There are no reports of the use of weapons in fights at the railway gates site and, in a later period when they do occur, community elders emphasised that this was not acceptable behaviour. A former tent boxer, Tom, once told me that the current generations 'wouldn't last five minutes with the old men who fought at the gates', due to their unwillingness to settle disputes the proper way.

Erambie people who witnessed them described how the fights at the gates brought disagreements to an immediate and proper end as the combatants became 'friends again'. What was described by outsiders in negative terms appears to have been a highly ritualised and very effective way of dealing with disputes. A number of meanings have been attached to the fights. The variation in these meanings can be seen in the language used to describe them. Erambie residents retained a unique form of dispute management to which we have attached a meaning that is linked to Wiradjuri identity.

No more fighting at the gates

Sylvia and Mavis were sitting on the veranda enjoying a cup of tea and chatting. Mavis was talking about a tribal fight at a site in Cowra where her great-grandmother was wounded by an errant spear. I sat on the edge of the veranda observing, when Sylvia began to tell me about a fight between two now-deceased men that she remembered watching at the railway gates site when she was a young woman. 'May, do you remember that?' she asked. Mavis confirmed that she did before Sylvia added, talking to me, 'the railway gates used to be the boxing ring where they settled their differences. Off the mission away from the manager's house'. 'Away from them so they wouldn't ring the *gunyans* [police],' Mavis said. 'It was always before nine o'clock and off the mission,' Sylvia continued, 'the manager, he'd call the coppers and say there was a riot on the mission. So that's probably why they had it at the railway gates'. Sylvia began to giggle at the memory, 'and you always knew there was a fight on, on a Sunday morning because there'd be a big — all the Kooris would be walking up toward, real slow, yarning, up toward the railway gates because,' she laughed, '[they] knew there was gonna be a fight'.

After a pause in the conversation Mavis asked how long the fights at the railway gates had been 'going on'. She asked Sylvia, who is her senior. They agreed that the fights at the railway gates spanned their life times. As the discussion went on the two women agreed that outsiders did not understand the fights and that the fights were held at that site as a compromise by community members who, Sylvia said, needed a way to 'resolve our differences'. 'That's what they call keeping it in house,' she added, 'you know, they went up there and they were free to do that. But the thing about the fights at the gates, they had a timekeeper and it was run properly like a real fight,' she laughed at the memory. 'Different to now,' Mavis said and Sylvia agreed. Mavis thought that the fights at the gates stopped when a certain generation of notable fighters and senior men passed away. 'And the managers left,' they agreed. Mavis worried that there were 'no more fights at the gates'. 'No more fights at the gates,' Sylvia repeated to end that topic and move the conversation on.

I have heard this story about fighting at the railway gates many times. Senior members of the community lament the end of those fights. To them, it was clearly an important tool for settling disputes within the community.

Josie talked about the fights at the railway gates at length. She remembered them fondly as she explained their value and meaning to the community. Josie's five older brothers were regulars in bare-knuckle fights and she played a role too:

> Well, if anyone had a few drinks and they had a squabble the night before they'd go up to the gates, they'd have a fight. Everyone was allowed to go up and have a look. No-one was allowed to butt in and interfere with the fight that was happening because people was there, if you said something about the fight you'd be asked to leave. So when you went up there it wouldn't matter if your brother or your father was fighting, your nephew, you had to keep quiet. No-one was getting mobbed because you had a proper referee and that person was the referee. You wasn't even to barrack for anyone of them who was fighting. You just had to shut your mouth and watch the fight. When the fight finished they shook hands and walked away as friends. If you barracked and went on, that'd start more or less a blue, and because they were fighting at the gates they wanted to get it out of their system, whatever happened, and that was the proper procedure. I thought whoever made that up was good because then they would still be fighting, so whoever fought up the gates would have a round or two and that's it. Well, I don't know if it started, it probably started before my time and then again it might not have, but the old railway gates is still there, like part of it you can see, there's no gates there but that's where they sort of had to, what do you call it, settle their difficults [sic] at the gates. I believe if they was caught on the mission fighting they'd get a fine, so if they fought up there, a sober fight, it was just as I pointed out, getting rid of their difficults [sic] and then they became friends. Living on Erambie when there was managers there [and] people wasn't allowed to even drink and if they got caught there they'd be either in jail or fined 20 pound. [If] you was fighting, the police would take you and you'd be gone to Bathurst [gaol] because you wouldn't have no money to pay your fine and they'd hit you with 20 pound if you was in the wrong or the right. They'd just go up and when they'd go up there they'd pick the referee. Well, who was gonna be the referee? They'd ask someone and if people didn't want to they'd

say no, and they'd ask, they'd stand up and say, 'yeah I'll do it, I'll referee'. And I remember up there, up the gates once my brother was fighting and I could see that [his opponent] wanted to break it up and I said, 'that's it now, finished', and he just took notice to me. No-one said nothing to me by even saying that, but I just asked him to stop it. I said, 'come on, finish it up', and I was a young woman then. I said, 'come on', I said, 'don't go fighting no more. Shake hands and finish it'. They shook hands and walked away but if it wasn't like, my brother, I wouldn't be able to say that to two other young men. But seen as he was my brother I had the rights to say finish it up. It was early in the morning. I used to go to work. Sometimes it would be Sunday mornings because they'd have a *binjaling* [fight] the night before. Ah, and then it would be mainly Sunday mornings they'd have a fight up there because Saturday nights used to be going out and when they'd go out they'd have a fight in the town or coming home they'd be fighting so then they, whoever thought they got a raw deal the night before, would pull the other one out. I knew he [her brother] was fighting because he said he was going to have a go. They was only young, he said, 'I'm going to pull him out'. I was just waiting for them to see if they was going to fight. I was supposed to go to work that morning, see, I used to work in town and I was on the bike. Well I hung around there to watch and when they, when they started to fight I rode up on the bike and when they finished then I rode to work. I wanted to have a look at them first…It was only, as I pointed out, the ones that thought they had a raw deal or they wanted to get if off their chest, then they become good friends.

I remember another fight up there at the gates. They had a fight, they was only young men and something happened, I think the night before, and they wanted to fight. Then, when they was fighting, my brother refereed and then I think one got over the other, and his [the loser's] uncles was there and said, 'well, now [you] belted him you can belt me'. I remember that as plain as yesterday and Bernie was the ref and he said, 'no'. 'No,' he said, 'he had a fight, so if you must have a fight, you fight me.' He wouldn't fight him and Bernie was a lot younger then too, and he said, 'I refereed the fight, he's had a fight and he's not fighting anybody else'. Because that wasn't fair, so they all walked away then. Then that's all he said to him, 'well look, he's just had a fight, the fight was fair and I refereed it and that's it. If you want a fight you'll have to fight me because he's not gonna fight someone who was just fighting'. See, that would have ended up into a big blue.

Josie used our word for a fight, *binjaling*. This is not uncommon. The English and Wiradjuri words for fight are often interchanged in this way. However, she was aware that she was potentially speaking to a wider audience than just myself when retelling the story above, and it did appear that she made this reference intentionally. By using *binjaling* in her account Josie was making a connection between the Erambie way of fighting and the past. Mavis remembered the fights in a similar way. Although she did indicate some temporary resentment between fighters from time to time, the overall message was that the fights resolved disputes:

> The gates was at the back of the mission, at the railway line. There was a road going to the houses that the Newtons lived in. When a train was coming the gates were closed. If two people had a fight on the mission they would say, 'I'll see you at the gates in the morning'. Both men and women fought at the gates. Most of the people from the mission went up to watch them fight. I don't remember any refereeing or rules. Both fighters just went punch for punch. The one that was winning would know when he had the other one beat and he would stop the fight and shake hands, there was no hate. They travelled with Sharman's boxing tent so they knew how to fight. The one that got beat went to the older boxers to show him how to fight better. The people would laugh when they seen the loser sparring around and say, 'look at him getting ready for another hiding'. The women went at it punch for punch. No pulling hair, they fought like the men. They would be angry for a few days and did not talk, then they made friends and forgot about the fight. Josie said the only rules was no double-banking [two people attacking one] and the women had to be quiet or leave.

Lachlan touched on his perceptions of the differences in the meanings attached to the fights by outsiders and those from within the community. He explained where he thought the fights came from and what they meant to him: 'What we had in them days was a great thing you know, up the gates… we all make mistakes then you go and say, "we'll go up the gates and we'll sort it out".' When I asked him why he thought they fought at the gates he linked the practice to community tradition:

> Because it was a tradition at that time, there was no fighting on the mission especially if you was drunk and no fighting in front of family. But it was a funny thing, because you don't fight in front of the family on the mission but when you go up to the gates they all followed you up anyways. At least they respected people's homes and that, you know, to not fight in front of someone's home…Same as here, if someone goes to fight out the front you know you wouldn't respect them. But if they go down the road and fight you'd walk down the road and watch them then.

Lachlan said that he did not know when or how the practice of fighting at the gates started but did remember being in attendance at fights in the 1940s. He also recalled fighting with other mission children while growing up and linked this with his later success as a boxer who toured Australia with the travelling boxing tents. This indicates that fighting was a constant part of his life on the reserve and he considered it normal for a man to fight.

Lachlan believed that the practice of fighting was 'linked back to our culture'. He told me, 'we had that type of thing where you get a killer boomerang or spear and come out and settle it one-on-one without involving the family'. Erambie elders consistently say that fighting is a valid dispute management technique that has carried over from our pre-contact culture. A common theme in the way Erambie community members remembered the fights at the gates was that they controlled and ended disputes, which made them valuable to the community. This type of dispute management would have been important for a community that lived so closely together, sometimes with two or three families living in one small house. This can be seen in Lachlan's statement about how the fights controlled disputes:

> It was a good way, if you got a dispute then everybody can talk over and over and over, everybody's got a point you know…And you could argue the point for days but now go up the gates and one-on-one, whoever won who lost — whatever, you go back and…well it's finished.

Lachlan was 'positive' that the managers reacted to stop the fights because they did not understand why and how the mission residents used fighting to settle even seemingly minor disputes. This is evident in his comment that I used to open this chapter, which indicates there was a valid reason why Erambie residents refused to allow the fights to be ended by outsiders. Given the focus of this chapter on these competing understandings of the fights at the gates, it may be useful to repeat Lachlan's words here:

> They [the managers] didn't understand the culture of our people, they didn't understand what the little biff or whatever was about. See, maybe I can align it to American states where they used to call it a duel where you go there with your one shot gun to protect your honour. You go out and take twenty paces, turn around and shoot each other. So I can sort of align our culture with that. But brother, they [white people] just didn't understand.

The managers were not alone in their condemnation of bare-knuckle forms of fighting. The loss of popularity of bare-knuckle fighting is attributed in part to the 'brutal and bloody' nature of the sport (Brailsford 1988: 2). Changes in the way bare-knuckle fighting was perceived according to changes in social and ethical expectations meant that 'pugs slipped too far away from the new', according to Brailsford (1988: 2). Boxing survived by accommodating the forced changes as it strove to maintain popularity and respectability. The changes involved safety considerations such as timed rounds and mandatory rests, along with padded gloves for the hands to reduce the severity of blows. The use of skin and padded gloves gained ground in the 1870s and helped to 'remove some of the distaste for boxing felt by the respectable elements', which included people from the churches, according to Corris (1979: 45). He also reported that bare-knuckle fighting 'lost ground as a social institution' around this time (1979: 48). At the time that Erambie residents were continuing to use bare-knuckle fighting to settle disputes, the practice was looked down upon by much of white society.

Community members' descriptions of the fights indicate that they involved precautions to ensure the safety of the participants. For example, the winner would usually bring the fight to an end when they saw that an opponent was beaten. The evolving rules of boxing were probably adapted to Wiradjuri fighting because they further contributed to safe fighting. Similarly, the fights described by Erambie residents were not characterised by the brutality of a 'blood sport' but as a highly ritualised and safe way of maintaining social order. Lachlan was adamant that fighting 'one out [one-on-one] is the best and fairest, the best way to go' in settling disputes. This is a consistent theme among senior Erambie people who even express disappointment that fights are no longer conducted in the proper way at the railway gates.

The managers' representations of the fights, on the other hand, were in line with the view that fighting was not an acceptable way to behave. They reported the fights as examples of negative behaviour that resulted from a breakdown of the ability to maintain order within the community. This had the effect of reinforcing their position as keepers of order for a community that could not do so for itself. The managers documented their views on the fighting on Erambie to a wider community in which many opposed bare-knuckle fighting as unacceptable behaviour.

Colonial societies took their lead from London in the early 1800s by looking on bare-knuckle fighting in two opposing ways (Walmsley & Kosuth 2000). The social reformers considered this type of fighting to be unique to the drunken underclass and the impoverished. In contrast, many drinking men regarded fights as 'acceptable' and even 'preferable' in settling disputes (Walmsley & Kosuth 2000: 419). Later, the link between drinking and fighting would be reinforced in the Erambie managers' reports. Associating the fights with drinking effectively portrayed them as negative behaviour. However, the members of the Erambie community spoke of 'having a sober go' at the gates without the use of alcohol. Even though the residents of Erambie did not see the fights as uncivilised, they were expected to change just as the pugilists in other colonised societies were changing.

To the Kooris at Erambie, however, fighting had been a social practice for an undated period of time before white people arrived. The fights at the railway gates were not conducted by drunken men but were used to restore order which may have been, in some instances, disrupted by drunken people. The people of Erambie used a range of strategies to continue the practice. These strategies ranged from ignoring intrusive attempts to stop fights to accommodating the managers by establishing a site outside their control. Despite the negative framing of the fights they remained acceptable to the residents. Introducing boxing rules and discarding weapons made the fights even safer. The fights usually involved kin who were concerned for the physical and emotional safety of all involved. When Josie remembered victorious fighters calling 'enough', this desire to not cause too much physical or emotional harm is clear. Mavis also remembered this feature of the fights in her account of fighting at the gates:

> They shake hands and say, 'I will see you at the gates in the morning'...I don't remember anyone refereeing, the two people that was fighting would go punch for punch and the person who was winning would end the fighting if he knew he had the other one beat. They shake hands...There was no hate between the fighters.

My earliest memories of the fights include running barefoot early in the morning so as not to miss a much anticipated fight. In a lifetime of watching these fights one thing that I have observed is the amount of 'show' they include. It appears to me that being willing to participate is an important element in the process. 'Fronting up' to defend the family or personal honour is an important factor for many and some even turn up at a fight and put on a show without actually fighting.

Compare the language used to describe the fights and the contrast between the points of view is apparent. Where the managers used terms such as 'riotous behaviour', 'lack of control', 'brawling' and 'danger', members of the Erambie community spoke of togetherness, 'settling disputes' and restoring friendship by 'sorting it out the right way'. Scholarly research has aligned the fights with pre-contact culture by writing about continuities and persistence. The difference in the understanding and representations of the fights comes from the differences in approach of the people who have represented the fights. The managers imposed their own concept of bare-knuckle fighting as to 'belong more to the primitive', whereas the mission residents considered that the practice of fighting to settle disputes belonged in the present and future (Brailsford 1988: 2).

These competing accounts illustrate the differences in the way people were informed about the fights within the Erambie community. On the one hand, the practice of fighting at the gates was considered by some to be evidence of a carry-over of Wiradjuri culture from the pre-mission era. Still others have represented the fights as evidence of cultural and social breakdown. Not all accounts of the fights are equal, however, and where and how the fights are presented has varied. Ultimately, the power to create knowledge about this cultural practice rested outside the community. The imbalance between oral and documentary sources meant that the fights were used to move the identity of the Wiradjuri further away from the authentic and more toward a hybridised culture. With the inclusion of Koori voices, the fights can be interpreted as linking the Erambie community more closely with the authentic Koori culture of the past. Fighting within the Erambie community is an example of continuity of culture and the people of Erambie value this type of physical activity partly for this reason.

Chapter 5

The Wiradjuri clever men

The clever men of south eastern Australia have indeed vanished and there is no possibility of their return. (Beckett, in Elkin 1977: xxi)

Oh mate, they was smart men. Very clever men. Oh mate, they was smart men. Very clever. (The Storyteller)

One reason for writing this book was to record the achievements of the athletes that I grew up idolising. The way the athletes of the Murray family were and are described illustrates the complex nature of identity construction. There is no single or unified representation of Aborigines presented in this book; however, the general picture that emerges from some portrayals that I discuss here is that Aborigines are inferior to Europeans. By contrast, the Murray athletes were described in the Cowra newspapers differently from other Erambie Aborigines. Because the Murrays were especially difficult for white people to understand through the prism of their negative stereotypes, representations of them became increasingly detached from Aboriginality.

Stuart Hall uses a constructivist approach to explain the language used to represent the 'other'. This approach focuses on the ways language constructs meaning. In the newspaper articles about the Murrays there is often an absence of the language used to describe other Aborigines. At no stage were the Murray athletes described in a way that indicates they were examples of good within the Wiradjuri community. By contrast, within the Erambie community members of the Murray family continue to be put forward as examples of what is good about our community and culture. I have employed Hall's use of Douglas' ideas about certain types of representations restoring order when 'matter is found out of place' to interpret the data in this chapter. The argument

I make is that the contrasting representations of the Murray family are used to maintain accepted social order in ways that are context dependant.

For some white people, the Murray family represented examples of Aborigines being 'out of place'. Over a seventy-year period, this talented family demonstrated the way sport and physical ability can be used to uphold accepted representations of Aborigines. My analysis includes identifying the way the Murrays were known within the community as well as outside of it. Conflict arose when these descriptions did not conform to general beliefs about Aborigines. The focus then shifts to the period when a change in thinking was forced by the unexpected survival of many Indigenous Australian communities. The meanings attached to the Murray family's abilities are highlighted in the constantly changing portrayals of these multi-talented men. Among the storytellers the Murray family is known in relation to representation and cultural survival.

Recognising the 'extraordinary'

During the nineteenth century inscribed metal gorgets, or 'king plates', were used to give recognition to certain Aborigines who most distinguished themselves in the eyes of the whites. Working to catalogue and record the history of king plates, Troy described how some white settlers devoted particular attention to prominent Aborigines in order to gain their co-operation (1993). However, Troy found that within their own clans, people were 'given only respect they earned within their own society' (1993: 21). Wiradjuri people gave special consideration to athletes and to '[t]he best fighting man' (Troy 1993: 96).

Working in the first half of the twentieth century, anthropologist Ronald Berndt made a more detailed record of the attributes of exceptional Wiradjuri men (1947). Wiradjuri men, born around the same time as Harry Murray, shared their knowledge of 'clever men' with Berndt:

> A Wuradjuri [Wiradjuri] native-doctor was called *wiri:nan* ('powerful man'); *bugi:nja* ('spirit', or 'spirit of the whirlwind') since it was the custom of his spirit-self to travel in a whirlwind; *ki:ka:wi:lan*, or more generally *walemira* [*walamira*], translated as 'the clever one'.

The word *walemira* meant not only clever in the ordinary manner of speaking, but also intellectually clever, and having the ability...to perform wondrous feats...He was also called *walemira talmai* (i.e. 'one to whom cleverness has been handed on', or 'the passing on of cleverness')...he was recognised as one of the 'intellectuals' of the tribe, and as a man who was socially of great value. It was possible for him to assume the chief headmanship...in this way he could become both temporal and spiritual leader of his group. Such an important position involved the accumulation of a great amount of prestige for himself, his family and his close relatives, which would however not develop in the individuals concerned any autocratic tendencies... informant stressed the fact that 'you could always tell a *walemira* no matter where you saw him'; the distinction from other men was not physical, but could be observed by the 'intelligent' light in his eyes which differed inexplicably from that of other men. Further, great doctors were said to have been enveloped in a peculiar atmosphere, which caused ordinary people to feel diffident in their presence. (Berndt 1947: 331–2)

Using the notes made by Berndt, his then research assistant, AP Elkin, described men who stood apart from others in his 1945 book *Aboriginal men of high degree*. Elkin defined the clever man as 'one who had been admitted to the secrets not disclosed to the ordinary' (1945/1977: xvii). His descriptions suggested that clever men were still recognised within Wiradjuri communities at that time. However, in the preface to the second edition of Elkin's book, published in 1977, anthropologist Jeremy Beckett declared the clever men of south-eastern Australia to be consigned to the past. Berndt, Elkin and Beckett focussed on the mystical or professional (such as medical) attributes of clever men and when they no longer observed these attributes they assumed that the clever men had died out. Aborigines have also attributed physical skills and leadership qualities to clever men and are therefore able to point to their continued existence.

In the third section of *Aboriginal men of high degree*, which he added for the second edition, Elkin questioned whether any clever men had survived. In doing this he made two important concessions. First, he recognised that the data he used to describe the attributes of clever men was 'inadequate' because the Indigenous informants were not inclined to share knowledge with those who had not earned that right. He also observed that he considered language differences to be a barrier to accurate communication. The second important concession he made was that, for questions about the survival of clever men, 'the answer will be given by the Aborigines themselves' (1977: xvii).

The Bidja

Harry Murray was the owner of a king plate and he was recognised as a leader among his people. According to his grandson Jim Murray, he had inherited the king plate and leadership within his clan. Harry Murray is also recognised among the Erambie Wiradjuri as the *bidja*, a leader or head man. Murray's family had been recognised as exceptional among their peers. Erambie people say that they were among the established leaders of the local Wiradjuri when white people settled in the area.

Harry Murray enhanced his family's reputation as exceptional by upholding Wiradjuri values. It is doubtful whether the Erambie community could have survived without him. He was an accomplished athlete, businessman, teacher and a respected leader who came from a line of Wiradjuri leaders. He was all of these things at a time when the prevailing racial attitude had low expectations of Aborigines. In fact, in the 1890s, Aborigines were expected to die out due to an assumed physical and mental inferiority (McGregor 1997; Russell 2001; Anderson 2002). This point is illustrated by a paper delivered at the Australian Association for the Advancement of Science meeting in 1890. The Vice-president of the Royal Society of Tasmania, James Barnard, argued that 'the inferior race of mankind must give place to the highest type of man' and that this law, the law of evolution and survival of the fittest, 'is adequate to account for the gradual decline in numbers of the [A]boriginal inhabitants of this country' (in McGregor 1997: 48–9). In this climate, missions and reserves were established to 'protect' and divide the Indigenous populations.

In many colonised countries during the late nineteenth and early twentieth centuries, the acceptance of aborigines into mainstream sports served to uphold white perceptions of democracy (Gems 1999). In the United States, the racist tenants of social Darwinism, upheld by the white media, offered different representations of Native Americans and African-Americans at different points in the colonisation process. For example, Native Americans, once they ceased being a threat to white society, could be seen as noble savages and primitives as opposed to the brutish African-Americans (Gems 1999). In the Australian context the expected demise of Aborigines helped to shift them from dangerous brutes to noble savages. It was into a climate of expected demise and qualified acceptance that Wiradjuri men Harry and Sam Murray, both in their mid-twenties, entered the Western District sporting scene in the late 1890s.[1] It is worth pointing out that in other parts of Australia at that time Aborigines would not have been allowed to compete (Tatz & Tatz 2000). This reminds us that people thought differently about Aborigines at different times and in different places.

The earliest recorded entry by the Murray brothers into Cowra's developing sporting scene was in 'athletic sports' races promoted by local businessmen in the late 1890s. The brothers dominated the handicap sprint races at the time despite giving competitors up to twelve yards start. In addition to competing in sprint races, both Murray brothers represented Cowra in local rugby football matches, with the *Cowra Free Press* (*CFP*) recording Sam as scoring tries in football matches during the late 1890s. From their early success as sprinters the brothers took different paths. While the younger and better performing Sam pursued sprinting as a career, Harry remained in the district and took an active role in establishing the Wiradjuri community on the newly formed Mulyan reserve in West Cowra.

The newspaper reports of Sam Murray's victories invariably made reference to his race as a marker of difference, as for example the following *CFP* article did when it implied a link between race and the running speed of the 25-year-old sprinter:

> The ridiculous ease with which that dusky son of the sod [Sam Murray] won the final in the principal handicap shows that his powers were considerably discounted by the handicappers. (20 April 1899)

The athletic reputation of the Murray family had its origins in the achievements of Sam Murray, but his career as a sprinter outside of Western District events was not widely covered in the *CFP*. Consequently, when he died at 35 from typhoid,[2] his achievements at the Stawell Gift may not have been widely known. However, within the Erambie community he has a place in the oral history tradition as a runner-up in the professional sprint race that became widely regarded as the most prestigious in the world. In fact, as the reputation of the Stawell Gift has grown, Sam Murray's story has gained more prominence within Erambie. Each Easter, as the race is held, stories about his success in the race are retold by family members or others who are familiar with it. He is also mentioned when his nephew Jim's running ability is talked about. The following account of Sam's near victory was published in the *Stawell News*:

> Nolan was very anxious to beat the gun, and failing had to go back a yard. At the second try the field was sent away as if by machinery. Clark was soon on even terms with Horswood, Nolan being next, with Murray and the favourite coming strong. Murray and McManus were only separated by a couple of feet about thirty yards from home, but Clark gamely threw off the challenge of the aboriginal and finally landed a winner by a couple of yards; Murray finished second, only a few inches in front of McManus. (4 April 1899)

Murray was identified as 'aboriginal' in the race review as well as the race program with an 'a' next to his name. Other Indigenous athletes, including Larry Marsh of Queensland, were also identified according to their caste. In the Stawell Easter Gift official program, which was also published in the *Stawell News* of 21 March, Sam was distinguished from half-castes ('h.c.') and other 'colored [sic] people' ('c.p.') such as Asians. In the final, the Stawell program reported that Murray conceded five yards start to the eventual winner and almost won the event. The report also described how he competed in the 220 yards race, the Steward's Purse Handicap, where he narrowly lost to NC Clark despite conceding him six yards start. By comparison, another noted Indigenous athlete, Larry Marsh, competed in this event as a backmarker (a runner who gave the rest of the field a head start) without making the final. Comparing Murray's performances against other well-known athletes gives an idea of his ability, achievements and form as a sprinter at the time.

Sam Murray followed the professional running circuit to compete in New South Wales and Victoria. For his second placing at Stawell he received seven pounds, just missing the seventy pounds winner's purse. One of the features of pedestrianism (professional running), then as now, is that the athletes and their backers can often make far more money by gambling on results than through prize money alone. Murray's win in the preliminary rounds of the Stawell Gift, for example, could have earned him more than his eventual runner's-up purse. His winnings from the Western District Sheffield Handicaps also represented a comfortable living at the time. In the weeks following his efforts at Stawell, for example, the *CFP* reported that he received one pound ten shillings for winning the Great Western Hotel Handicap over 100 yards, and his brother Harry collected the other ten shillings on offer by finishing second. Again, Aboriginality was mentioned in the newspaper report of this race when Sam was described as 'that dusky son of the sod' (20 April 1899).

As I have noted earlier, being the son of a leader in Wiradjuri society does not mean automatic acceptance as a leader. Harry Murray senior, Sam's brother, earned his position among the Cowra Wiradjuri through his athletic ability and his activism on behalf of the Erambie community. Although he may not have been as athletically gifted as Sam, he excelled in a number of areas. Senior men and women at Erambie recount his many talents and achievements when they speak of the Bidja of Erambie. I was told how he operated a successful business and was instrumental in establishing the Erambie community. In addition, Murray was known to be a talented entertainer.

From the early 1890s and even after the appointment of a white manager by the Aborigines Protection Board in 1924, Murray used his education to act as a spokesperson in dealings with the white community. He raised objections when the *CFP* reported stories that he felt were false or negative about the community. In July 1923, the *CFP* reported that Murray had objected to a newspaper report that an Aborigine convicted of a crime was from the mission (10 July). The *CFP* also reported in 1926 that the 'uncrowned king' of the mission resisted attempts by the Board, fuelled by complaints from the Cowra community, to relocate the reserve 20 miles from the town (28 May). These are stories that are part of the living oral history of Erambie.

Harry Murray's great-granddaughter, Mary Coe, made the point that 'chiefs' continued to be part of Wiradjuri culture even though their role had changed to include leadership in battles for civil rights. Coe writes: 'There have been a great many Aboriginal leaders since the days of Windradyne right up to the present and they are continuing the fight for Koori people's rights' (1989: 83).

Being the leader of the community often put Murray in a position of conflict with white authorities. For example, just two years after being appointed to Erambie Mission in 1924, a manager attempted to have the Murray family expelled from the reserve because he constantly clashed with Harry Murray. The *CFP* reported that the attempted expulsion came after one incident where Murray 'took strong exception' to attempts by the manager, Constable, to regulate access to the mission (28 May 1926). The reputation of the Murray family in the town, along with their membership of the Australian Labor Party, led to a public inquiry into the incident. The *CFP* report on this incident gives an indication of how attempts were made to manage the Wiradjuri identity of a man who did not fit the accepted stereotype of Aborigines. Constable attempted to discredit Murray by claiming that he did not deserve the reputation he enjoyed in the town. The article included an overview of Harry Murray's position in the community:

> It appears that Harry Murray, who has a reputation for being the 'uncrowned King' of the local aborigines, made a complaint to local members of the A.L.P. that he and his family were being unjustly treated by the manager of the Erambie Mission (Mr. Constable). As the family referred to are strong Labour [sic] supporters the local branch deemed it its duty to have an investigation. (28 May 1926)

Under the section heading, 'Murray bears a good character in Cowra', eight townspeople described him as a 'clean living' and 'honest' man. By contrast, the Board argued that Murray did not 'behave' himself in return for the 'comforts' they provided. A supporter of Murray from the Cowra community then said, 'I've heard complaints from others beside the Murrays, but probably they do not say so to you', a reminder that Murray was speaking on behalf of the community.

Later in the article, the Murrays asserted their position within the community. Jane Murray is reported to have said 'excitedly', '[w]e are the original owners. The reserve was granted to the Murray family by Minister Jobson'. When Mr Donaldson, the Board representative, stated that he only wanted Harry Murray to 'conform to the rules', Murray reportedly replied, '[w]hat is wrong with my conduct?' It is this defiant attitude towards the injustices of white authority that dominates stories Erambie people tell about Harry Murray.

The stories I have heard about Harry and Jane Murray focus on their position as a long established family in the area and the respect the people had for them. Harry Murray's son-in-law recalled:

> Everyone seemed to look to the Murrays. If they wanted anything they were the first people to go to. If they wanted to know anything, they'd be there…She was a lovely old lady, and they used to ask her for money, and she'd give it to them. Ask for food, she'd give it to them, and all that sort of business. She never let any of them down. (in Read 1983: 14)

Lachlan noted Murray's position within the community:

> The people would go and tell Mr Murray, and he'd tell Mr Constable [the first manager of Erambie station]. He'd tell him, he wouldn't hesitate. He never ever swore, you know. He said 'you can't stand over my people'. (in Read 1984a: 14)

Sylvia remembered other members of the Murray family fondly. She often talked about Harry's daughter Ollie Murray being a beautiful singer, and how Doolan Murray was 'so talented'. She described some of the Murray family: 'They'd leave these young fellas for dead. Uncle Major played the piano-accordion, poor old Gertie Mac's [Harry Murray's eldest daughter] place was the place they pushed the partition back and they'd have a dance.' Sylvia also remembered with great pride that: 'Poor old Janey Murray brought me into the world. She's on my birth certificate. She was one of the nicest ladies you could ever wish to meet.' The *CFP* reported that Mrs Murray had objected to the mission manager's wife 'making reference to the uncleanly state of some of the children' (28 May 1926). The state of children's clothing and cleanliness was an important issue for mission residents who lived with a constant threat of having children removed. The idea of cleanliness is a recurring theme in the stories told about life under the Board. Objecting to judgements being made by the manager's wife undoubtedly added to Jane Murray's status among mission residents. It is a further example of the Murray family acting as advocates for the community.

Even though she was not old enough to remember Harry or Jane Murray themselves, Josie remembered the stories about them:

> They used to always talk about Harry and Janey Murray when we was growing up. They was around before my time. They always talked about them because living under the white managers' system they used to see that people more or less had a fair go.

Indigenous rights campaigner Bill Ferguson claimed that the attempt to remove Harry Murray led to 'unease' between Erambie residents and outsiders that was still evident in 1929 when he spent time on the reserve (in Horner 1994: 26). Ferguson praised the Murrays and noted that they had 'been famous athletes for generations' (in Horner 1994: 26). The sporting ability of the Murray family contributed to them earning a reputation both within the Erambie community and among Europeans.

Having this reputation meant that the Murrays did not conform to the accepted way Aborigines were represented and this in turn led to attempts to manage them and their identity. Perhaps personal contact with outsiders through sport negated attempts to discredit the family. Moreover, within the Erambie community the attacks against the Murrays served to reinforce the reputation of the family and their identity as Wiradjuri clever men. The Protection Board's attempts to manage the identity of the Murray family when it tried to expel them was not the last time it sought to explain the Murrays in terms of prevailing racial thought.

'Cowra's sensation: The redoubtable Doolan Murray'

After Sam and Harry, the Murray name did not reappear in the local sports pages again until Harry's 18-year-old son Herbert John, better known as Doolan, emerged as an all-round athlete in 1915. Doolan was the most prominent of the six brothers who performed on the local and national sporting stage for three decades. The *CFP* recorded how he emulated his father, who acted as his trainer, by competing in local sprint races as a backmarker (26 May 1915). He also played rugby football for Cowra Federals as early as 1915 (*CFP* 2 June 1915), and when he entered the local boxing scene as a preliminary fighter his father accompanied him as a trainer and promoter. Although he excelled locally at a number of sports, it was as a boxer that Doolan gained wider recognition. His skill in the ring further enriched his family's reputation as talented and honourable people.

The newspaper descriptions of Doolan Murray contributed to his status as a local sporting idol. However, it is noticeable that the positive portrayals of Doolan Murray the boxer are not consistent with the negative way Aborigines generally were represented. There were also occasions when Doolan's identity was questioned and in some articles attempts were made to 'negrofy' him. In fact, in some instances Doolan was not talked about as an Aborigine at all. Overall, he was represented in ways that contrasted ideas put forward about Aborigines, such as those of the mission managers. By contrast, many Erambie residents speak about Doolan's achievements as examples of the existence of clever men.

In 1916 the *CFP* recorded Doolan's debut on the local boxing scene when, as a talented preliminary boxer, he 'shaped well' to win in front of a full house (29 April). The *CFP* described his next bout in 1917 when he gave a four-round exhibition spar, again as a preliminary to another featured fight. His father's 'mission entertainers' were also on the program for this event and were 'very much enjoyed by the audience' (14 March).

By January 1918 the *CFP* described him as 'nimble' and 'a little out of the ordinary as a boxer' (16 January). Doolan continued to play football for the Cowra Athletic Club rugby team and 'played well' before his departure 'for fresh fields' in 1918, which, the *CFP* said, would 'considerably weaken the Athletic Club's team' as he was 'always a safe fullback' (10 July).

A year later he re-appeared on the local sporting scene when the *CFP* reported that, as a backmarker, he was runner-up in the six-pound St Raphael's Handicap over 110 yards (11 June 1919). Then, in early 1920, he had his first headline bout in Cowra when he defeated the welterweight champion of the Australian navy for 35 pounds. The fight was staged in a specially constructed outside venue because of local interest. Doolan was becoming prominent as a local sporting identity. In the lead-up to the fight his growing reputation was reported in the *CFP* (20 January 1920). He won four of six bouts by knockout, one of his knockouts coming after just fifty seconds.

Doolan next headlined a boxing event at a packed Centennial Hall in Cowra. The *CFP* published the following account of the fight:

The big fight. Murray being the first to enter the ring and as he did so he received a great reception. The weights were announced as Murray 9.6 and Pollard 9.8. Murray was full of confidence and was in great condition, while Pollard, who did not look so well, was very determined. The first round commenced with a few smart punches being delivered by both men, but after it had been in progress for about 90 seconds Murray sent a beautiful right to the jaw which floored Pollard, who took the full count…Murray is undoubtedly a clever fighter and should be matched with some top notchers as he is sure to 'make good'. Some of our local sports who are prepared to back him claim 'Doolan' as a coming champion. Promoter Ted Hurst is in communication with Herb Sullivan (Sydney) and 'Kid' Harris with a view to arranging a match for Murray on March 10th…a record house should result. (28 February 1920)

After showing promise in local fights, Doolan Murray's backers brought more accomplished boxers from bigger cities to fight him in Cowra. On 13 March 1920, the *CFP* published a detailed account of Doolan's victory in a fifteen-round fight with New Zealander James 'Kid' Harris, which took place in front of the promised large crowd:

'House full' was the comment of Promoter Ted Hurst when 'Kid' Harris and 'Doolan' Murray shook hands prior to their fifteen round encounter at Centennial Stadium…and those who attended received well over their money's worth…When the gong sounded both men went for all they were worth and some exciting rallies followed…A challenge was at once issued by George Reidy, on behalf of Rutherford of Orange, to fight the winner for a purse of £50. It was accepted by Jimmy Hill, on behalf of Murray.

Doolan's next fight represented a further advancement in his career and it led to a bout 'with one of Sydney's cleverest lightweights' (*CFP* 10 April 1920). The *CFP* report of his victory over 'Buck' Shaw indicated that Doolan had a growing reputation as an entertaining fighter who was further developing his following among local fight fans:

A crowded house witnessed the second big pugilistic fixture of the season...and the man who says he did not see his money's worth is indeed a glutton for 'stoush'. A couple of preliminaries first occupied the attention of the big crowd. 'Doolan' Murray's two younger brothers showed great promise in their respective bouts...There was loud applause when the popular local idol, 'Doolan' Murray, accompanied by his seconds Williams and Joe Newham, stepped into the ring...the fight was willing from the word 'go'...Shaw did most of the leading, but he failed to connect on numerous occasions, thus losing many points, and frequently when his blows did find their mark Murray returned same with interest. Referee Thomas' decision was a good one, and was received with loud applause. (10 April 1920)

Next, Doolan met Alec Cowan of Port Kembla in March 1922 at Bourke's Stadium in Cowra. The reporter noted Doolan's sporting character in this fight. Such praise for the character of an Aborigine was not common at this time. Notice the way that Doolan is represented as the hero in this report from the *CFP*:

> Bourke's Stadium was crowded on Thursday night, the principal attraction being the best of 15 rounds between the local champion, Doolan Murray, and Alec Cowan, of Port Kembla...the latter appeared to be much heavier...Murray, showing much cleverness in evading punishment, getting in good work with the left. Early in the fourth, Cowan, with a left hook, sent Murray to the boards, but he rose at the count of eight, fresh and eager for more...In the ninth Murray gave his opponent a severe gruelling, whom he sent to the boards; Cowan immediately rose to his hands and knees, Murray sportingly retired a few paces and allowing him to regain the perpendicular; Murray then looked like finishing his man off, but the gong saved...Murray had the misfortune of breaking his right hand, but pluckily fought on... [the] decision...a draw — met with general approval. (18 March 1922)

Doolan fought often as he rose through the ranks of Australian lightweight boxers. The *CFP* followed his career closely and regularly reported on his progress. The growing number of articles claimed Doolan as one of their own. This was happening even at the time when the newspaper was at pains to identify the differences between the white people of Cowra and the blacks of Erambie. Doolan was subtly being separated from his kin in these articles. In contrast to the Erambie residents who were arrested for fighting, at no stage was Doolan written about in the *CFP* as representative of Aborigines.

After the fight with Cowan, Doolan again made a step up in class when he met 'Snowy' Hill of Sydney in a twenty-round contest. Hill had matched top-rated Australian Billy Grime before losing on a fifteenth-round foul four months earlier. The *CFP* reported that Doolan's hand injury from his fight with Cowan was not as bad as feared and 'Doolan says he is fit and well' for the trip to Forbes for the contest (22 March 1922). In the build-up to the fight, Doolan was 'billed as the Cowra sensation' (*CFP* 5 April 1922). With just ten days rest, he was matched with this tough and accomplished fighter:

> A very large crowd assembled at Ike Jacobs' Stadium last night to see Doolan Murray (billed as the Cowra 'sensation') and 'Snowy' Hill, of Sydney, meet. A good contest was anticipated, and those who attended were not disappointed, as up to the eighth round the points were fairly even, but slightly in favour of Murray, who was the favourite. In the 8th round the end came, Murray going down as a result of a blow which appeared to catch him low down. A 'foul' was at once claimed and at the count of 'six' Murray rose to his feet claiming a 'foul'. The referee ordered him to box on and as he refused the fight was awarded to Hill. The crowd received the decision very badly, and roundly hooted the referee…Murray was later examined by a doctor, who stated there was evidence of his having been struck low. He is now in Forbes hospital, but is not seriously injured. (*CFP* 5 April 1922)

Doolan returned to the ring eleven days later when he was matched with well-performing American Charlie 'Kid' Moy, a younger but far more experienced boxer. Moy had more than ninety fights in the United States and Australia to his credit, far more than Doolan at this stage. Among Moy's victims was Australian bantamweight champion, Billy Grime. On 19 April 1922 the *CFP* reported under the headline, 'Murray defeats Moy':

> Doolan Murray, the local champion added the scalp of another of the 'gun' boxers to his girdle on Friday night, when he outpointed the redoubtable American, Charlie Moy, before a packed house at

> Bourke's Stadium…in open work Murray more than held his own — in fact at times he made the Yank look like a mere novice…Prior to the big fight Jim Stanley and Claude Murray gave a clever sparring exhibition…Vince Pollard and Doolan Murray have been matched to fight here at an early date for £25 aside.

After the Moy fight Doolan's potential as a boxer was considered in the *CFP*, with the consensus that he was capable of competing against the best in his class.

> Jack Lynch, the well known Sydney boxing mentor, is of the opinion that Doolan Murray would make good with most of the cracks in his class 'down under', and that opinion is shared by a large number of Doolan's supporters in Cowra. Some even going so far as to say that he would not be outclassed by [Filipino champion] Jamito. (22 April 1922)

Doolan's victories over well-performing fighters brought him attention from Sydney. On 29 April 1922, a report by a Sydney boxing writer, 'Boxer Major', was included in the *CFP*:

> Doolan Murray, the abo lightweight, is described as a natural fighter who has been trained and lives in the aboriginal camp. 'A quick mover, very shifty, a good fighter, gritty as any white', is how a[n] [observer] described the dusky Native. There has been a lot of talk about Murray's weight and he has been credited, by men he has licked, as anything up to 11 stone. The [matter] was definitely settled the day [of] his fight with Snowy Hill, at Forbes when he was put on the scales and drew 9st 5½ pound. Stan Love (whom Doolan defeated at Coota.) and Fred Smith have been matched to fight at Wagga Friday night next for the State Lightweight championship.

Note how the Sydney press linked Doolan to supposedly 'white values' when they noted his 'gritty' character, the implication being that white people were inherently stronger of character than Aborigines.

Doolan Murray's next fight, against Australian lightweight champion Ern Baxter of Lithgow, was also publicised in the Sydney media. The *CFP* reprinted an article promoting the fight which was to be held at the famous Sydney Stadium:

Thus the Sydney sporting journal 'Box-On': — Ern Baxter and Doolan Murray meet at the Stadium on Monday, May 22nd. Murray is the wonderful Cowra aboriginal light-weight, and is termed the 'light-weight champion of the West'. (13 May 1922)

A week later the *CFP* announced that Doolan was to have his first fight in the 'big time' when he met Baxter:

Wednesday's 'Sun' contains a good portrait of Doolan Murray, who is to have his first fight in the 'big smoke' on Monday night, when he will be opposed by Ern. Baxter, the hard hitting Lithgow lightweight. (20 May 1922)

The *CFP* published the result of Doolan's loss to Baxter without a detailed account of the fight. It was reported that 'Murray fought well' in a fight that 'went the full 20 rounds' (24 May 1922). When Baxter was later knocked out by Jimmy Ryan, the *CFP* reported on 21 June that Doolan was matched with Ryan at the Hippodrome on 3 July 1922. There is no record that this fight took place and Doolan's only other recorded bout for 1922 was on 28 October, when the *CFP* recounted how he had knocked out 'ex-champion of the North' Sid Pascoe in the seventh round at the Globe Stadium in Cowra.

Doolan was supported in the ring by his father and other Erambie men. However, his managers or backers were white businessmen from Cowra who arranged and promoted his fights. One backer, Dan Gleeson, arranged another fight with Ern Baxter in addition to seeking further bouts with well-performing fighters. The *CFP* reported that 'Mick Hawkins, trainer of the late Les. Darcy, will probably bring a lad here to meet Murray' (13 January 1923). Doolan's record of sixteen fights resulted in eleven wins (six knockouts) and two draws.

On 20 February 1923 a report on the rematch with Baxter, taken from the *Lithgow Mercury*, was printed in the *CFP* under the headline: 'Cowra's champion beaten' in an 'interesting 20 round contest'. Although beaten, Doolan received generous praise for his fighting ability: 'Murray received an ovation for making Baxter miss badly with both hands. Murray tried his utmost to place a knock-out blow during the last couple of rounds, but the local boy was far too shifty'.

Doolan combined his boxing and football careers. He captained the Erambie football team during the period when they were travelling to games throughout the district and made a number of appearances for other local football teams such as the Cowra Rovers. His only other fight for 1923 was in August at Blayney against Horace Lee, an emerging lightweight at a stadium 'packed with men', many of whom found vantage points on the roof cross beams. The *CFP* published the following account of the fight:

> [T]he darkie was very clever on his feet and...smart with both hands... It was a lively scrap...[Doolan] Murray v Lee. The weights were given as Lee 10.5 and Murray 9.6, in the ring, but there looked to be even more difference than that...but Murray is a good general and taking the centre of the ring forced his opponent to fight from the ropes as well as keeping him continually on the move...it must be remembered it was his first fight of consequence and that he was opposed to a cool and resourceful boxer in Murray, who has beaten good men in the ring. (14 August 1923)

After the Lee fight, Doolan did not return to the boxing ring until 1924 when he accepted the challenge of Lithgow boxer Keith Gardiner for 25 pounds plus a percentage of the gate takings, on Easter Monday night. The *CFP* reported that Gardiner's backers thought he could defeat the 'Cowra champion' and accused his supporters of being 'slow to toe the line' in arranging wagers on the result (18 April 1924). The *CFP* reported Doolan's win:

> The Globe Stadium was crowded with boxing fans on Monday night... The main event, 20 rounds, between Keith Gardiner, of Lithgow, and 'Doolan' Murray, of Cowra was fought in a clean and sportsmanlike manner over the whole distance...Murray had Gardiner on the back-pedal throughout and was relying on aggressive and forceful tactics to gain him the points...we saw Murray fighting with some of his old time vim and dash and making Gardiner realise that he had struck a real snag...Murray was too powerful and had Gardiner on the floor for six. Both men were greeted with salvos of applause as the gong went... but Murray was always a slight bit better...running out a winner by a good margin. It was a good clean fight and Gardiner proved himself a

game lad and likely to hand a dangerous wallop at any time. He fought a great uphill battle against his stronger opponent. The decision in favour of Murray was well received. (24 April 1924)

Although he won the fight handily, this was the first time any newspaper reports had mentioned Doolan's age as being evident. The 'old time vim and dash' referred to Doolan's early career and to his recent losses. Even though he was 27, he had fought often in what was at the time a more brutal sport than it is now. Still, he continued to draw crowds and the repeated knock downs of Gardiner were reminiscent of the early days of his career eight years before. The 'Cowra champion' next took on a heavy-hitting fighter from Dubbo for 'a substantial side bet'. The *CFP* described the fight:

> A fair crowd assembled at the Globe Stadium last night, the main attraction being a fifteen round contest between Doolan Murray, the Cowra champion, and Dick Miranda, of Dubbo…Miranda appeared to have a decided advantage in poundage. Both lads showing remarkable cleverness and after fifteen rounds had been fought, referee Ted Thomas declared a draw. That decision met with a mixed reception. (6 June 1924)

Doolan returned to the Allblacks football team until September when 'the well known trainer of boxers, Pat McHugh', brought Reg Anderson from Sydney to fight him. The *CFP* reported that McHugh had brought fighters to Cowra to meet Doolan on two previous occasions without success (2 September 1924). At this stage of his career Doolan was matched with a number of emerging lightweights from Sydney and Western District towns. His reputation and experience made him a sought-after opponent for developing fighters. In 1925 a local poet and sports fan, Dick MacDonald, contributed a poem to the *CFP* that illustrated the reputation the Murray family had developed in boxing. The poem suggests the Murrays had overcome some prejudice with their sporting ability. 'As sport and man whether white or black' Doolan was to be revered, and readers were asked to '[d]rink to the Murrays …who box' (13 February 1925).

By 1927 the local press gave the impression that Doolan's career was in a decline as the *CFP* wrote reflectively about the man and his fight record. The *CFP* described how he had been 'too good for a fighter named Fitzgerald in their April bout at the Cowra Stadium' (22 April 1927). Then, in May of

1927, Doolan had a rematch with Dick Miranda. At this stage of his career the newspaper articles were saying that his fights were predominately organised to advance his opponents' careers as tests of skill and a chance to learn. However, this fight was fought in front of a crowded house and was billed in the *CFP* as 'the middleweight championship of the west':

> ...The fight was a particularly clean one. As a matter of fact there were occasions when both men acted in such a gentlemanly fashion as to give one the impression that they were not over anxious to unduly punish each other. Doolan smiled at Dick, and Dick smiled at Doolan. However, the next minute they would be going their hardest, and though Miranda landed many blows which Doolan took without a flinch, Doolan failed to connect with vicious right swings and upper cuts, which, had they landed appeared to have sufficient force behind them to send any ordinary man into slumber land...it was a clever exhibition of boxing on the part of Miranda, against an opponent, who is, without doubt, an infinitely better fighter. (17 May 1927)

In July of 1927 he lost a decision to a 'much heavier' opponent even though Doolan had knocking him down twice. Despite the decline in his career Doolan remained popular and the *CFP* continued to represent him in glowing terms. On 17 February 1929 the newspaper informed its readers that the 32-year-old Doolan Murray had 'his training quarters' at Mandurama where he was preparing to fight at Bathurst.

Doolan headlined many of tent-boxing legend Jimmy Sharman's shows during Sherman's visits to Cowra. On 10 September 1929 the *CFP* promoted Sharman's upcoming show with a profile of 'our local champion'. The newspaper described this show as 'the best two bobs worth I've ever seen':

> The splendid showing of our little colored [sic] boxer, 'Doolan' Murray, impressed all. Doolan is still capable of trading punches with any his weight, as was proved in a £10 challenge match against Jordan, of Coonamble. The points scored by Jordan were overshadowed by Doolan's heavy hitting, which floored Jordan three times. The decision displeased Jordan and his supporters; he has since challenged Murray for another match, and if completed they will meet in a special contest tomorrow (Saturday) night. (13 September 1929)

This next fight with Jordan was Doolan's last recorded fight in the *CFP*. Under the headline: 'Murray's Knockout', Doolan was apparently finishing with the same devastating fighting style that characterised his early career:

> Of the many excellent boxing and wrestling thrills given large crowds by the deservedly popular Jimmy Sharman Troup during carnival week a match between two Western District rivals, fought on Wednesday night between Doolan Murray (our local champion[)] and George Jordan (of Coonamble) caused much interest. The decision of Jim Flett was given to Murray, much to the dissatisfaction of the Far Western boxer and his supporters. The result was another match was arranged for a purse of £10, fought on Saturday night. The battle provided an excellent contest, in which both punched one another severely, the colored [sic] lad 'kidded' groggy in the 5th round, which caused the Coonamble fighter to think he had victory within his grasp, and in an unguarded moment Doolan drove a terrific right cross square to the chin, which resulted in one of the cleanest knockouts seen in these parts. Murray's win proved very popular. (13 September 1929)

The second fight with Jordan is Doolan's last recorded bout. Doolan relocated to the Riverina area of New South Wales with his family and eventually lived out his life there. The *Griffith Area News* included a summary of his sporting career in an obituary:

> For many years Murray was a trainer with the Cowra Group 9 Rugby League Club, however, he will be better remembered in Griffith as a keen boxing fan and in his younger days built up an excellent reputation as a boxer himself. He reached the stage of being a contender for the Australian lightweight title, the holder being Ern Baxter. (16 September 1973)

Doolan Murray was a honourable man who was known for his sportsmanship at a time when Aborigines were supposedly lacking such attributes. He was differentiated from his kin on the mission by newspaper reporters who described him as a kind of honorary white man because of the courage and sense of fair play he displayed. While his success was celebrated, he was written about in a way that linked him to 'white values'. Doolan's character was, in effect, disconnected from his Wiradjuri heritage. While Erambie Wiradjuri charged with offences were continually held up as typical of the social degeneration of Aboriginals, Doolan was not seen by outsiders as representative of Aborigines at all.

This analysis sits comfortably with Fanon's idea that colonised people are elevated above their 'jungle status' in proportion to their 'adoption of the mother country's cultural standards' (Fanon 1952/1970: 14). For the newspaper reporters it was not conceivable that Doolan was demonstrating the cultural standards of his Wiradjuri people. Mavis summed up what Erambie people say about the man:

> They [Erambie community elders] all used to share and help one another. He [Doolan Murray] had all his family there. Poor old Edie, poor old Moodie was related to him, Percy, poor old Gertie and all their kids. Ollie. He had a big family and we all shared things. That's a black thing, helping family like that.

Mavis linked Doolan's stature and character to Wiradjuri ways of acting, rather than white ways as claimed in the *CFP*. Erambie people often tell stories about people who 'left' the community to live with white people and 'wanted nothing to do with their people'. Remaining a part of the community at a time when being an Aborigine came with racism and restrictions is a marker of character to Erambie's people. By not leaving his people when he had the means and opportunity to do so, Doolan increased his standing within the community. Mavis said:

> He never lived with white people, he lived on the mission and when he went to Griffith he lived at the Three Ways [a Wiradjuri community near the town]. He was always living in blacks' camps. He was always with his people. He never left us, so that tells you something. What I can remember of Aunty Ethel and Uncle Doolan is that they had a nice house but they shared everything.

Mavis became slightly agitated when reading the quotes from the *CFP* and flatly denied that Doolan's character was anything other than a demonstration of Wiradjuri values:

That's not true. If he wanted to act like them he would have gone out and bought a house and cars, [material] things, like they [white people] do. Whenever he made money from fighting he used it to help his people. The elders like the Murrays were leaders of their people. They used music and singing and dancing and that to entertain and teach the kids. The leaders were respected because they acted like our ancestors not like whites…They gained respect by acting black not acting white. The leaders that were respected were the ones that acted like our people.

The white press contributed to Doolan's status as a sporting idol. They then claimed him as one of their own ('Cowra's champion') while associating his character with values supposedly only held by white people. In contrast, within the Erambie community he is talked about as an example of what is good about Wiradjuri people. He is talked about as the gentle Doolan who protected people in the community and is still admired as a Wiradjuri leader.

Despite being prominent in the community's catalogue of stories, the Murray men were not the only people described as clever. Other Erambie men and women were also admired when they demonstrated the abilities and values that were prized by Erambie people. Those who demonstrate these abilities and values are often described as clever and they are spoken of with great respect. Josie spoke about the high opinion she has for her 'aunties and uncles':

> I used to call them aunty and uncle. Buffalo Whitty was one elder that I looked up to. I remember Claude Murray [Doolan's brother]. He used to be always looking after the kids, always minding them and being very protective of them. That old fella, he died in 1953…He was always minding people's kids, walking around the mission with them. I always remember him, and Major Murray [Doolan's brother] was a handsome looking man.

Mavis added that another one of Doolan's brothers, Foley Murray, took great pride in his appearance. Josie described the people she remembered:

> …Poor old Buffalo Whitty he was a real good fighter that didn't like people to be stood over and then there was another old lady that I remember, Aunty Gertie McGuinness [Doolan's sister] she was

a fighter too. Then you had Edie Coe [another of Doolan's sisters] was another one. Then you had Aunty Nuggo Ingram and my sister Rebecca Bamblett who used to stand up out front [as leaders]. I used to watch them and I can remember Florence Wallace and Josie Whitty, they were people who would stand up and be counted when need to be, and have their say. Growing up the way we did on Erambie didn't worry me because all the people cared and shared for one another and helped one another. I used to take notice of my elders and how they used to talk and react when things happened and when I grew up I thought well, I'm going to go out and do what me aunties and uncles did. Major Murray I remember him. He was a quiet man. He more or less kept to himself…He had a hut. It was one of the nicest little tin huts they had on Erambie because he got out and fixed it up. He was middle aged then and I was still at school…If you mucked up or whatever people used to be there to keep you in line and other elders were allowed to keep you in line. They [community elders] were protective of our black kids and I was proud that I was one of them up there.

Gus and Brian spoke favourably of their elders in comparison to the managers. Both men condemned the mission managers and police as immoral while praising Erambie men as being moral. They retold a story about their memories of managers. Brian recalled his childhood memories of one particularly hated manager who 'used to walk around with them two big dogs, like Dobermans they was, real big dogs. And he'd tell the people what to do, "clean that yard up". He'd tell them what to do. Walking around with them big dogs all the bloody time'. Gus added, 'we hated them dogs, if you had to go over to his place to get rations or something you'd wait at the gate. Worried they might bite'. Brian followed this memory with his experience of clever men. He told a story of an encounter with such men while travelling for work:

When I was laying in me tent at night I heard pebbles hitting the tent roof. Boomp, boomp, boomp, you know. I lay there, still, until the next morning and when we [he and his co-workers] got up all of our food was gone. A featherfoot [a clever man] had come an' took all the food. That happened a few times too.

Brian spoke about a number of characteristics attributed to clever people within Koori communities and in doing so expanded the definition of the term. He talked about the elders whom he remembered from the mission as being kind and caring clever people and added that some of them (such as a featherfoot) were to be feared. He was making explicit a connection that had often been made implicitly when Erambie people spoke about their elders. The Wiradjuri people of the mission era are considered to be a continuation of the clever people from pre-invasion Wiradjuri culture. Erambie men and women earn respect when they demonstrate values considered important to the community. Sharing, and their willingness and ability to fight, are two of the more important values. No matter how much they engage with introduced vices such as alcohol, they will be respected as long as they can maintain these values.

There is a clear difference between the way that white people and Erambie Wiradjuri talk about people like Doolan Murray. With few exceptions, the white people generally represented Aborigines in negative ways. On the other hand, within their community, the Erambie elders were to be admired for their willingness to stand up for what they saw as right even if it meant having to fight. Men and women could be considered 'clever' if they demonstrated the abilities and values held dear within the community.

Brothers of the redoubtable Doolan

Doolan's brothers also continued the family's legacy as athletes. Their achievements in sport contributed to the way the family is represented within the Erambie community today. Frank, Major and Alan Murray were talented football players. The *CFP* described Major as '[a] player of no mean order' and '[a] man worthy of a place in any country team'. Claude partially emerged from Doolan's shadow as a boxer to become 'Cowra's coming champion' (1 May 1925). Claude relocated to Sydney where he fought professionally. A 1927 Bathurst *National Advocate* advertisement for a **Claude Murray** main-event fight at Bathurst promoted him as the **coming champion and the** fight report introduced him as Doolan's brother. The continued reference to the relationship between the Murrays no doubt contributed to the family's reputation as athletes. These positive reports also established a contrast between the way the Murray family were represented compared to other Aborigines. Under the headline, 'Murray outs Wilson', the *CFP* continued its positive portrayals of the Murray family when it described Claude's victory:

> Claude Murray, (9.0), brother of Doolan Murray, the Cowra black, made a decidedly good impression before a good house in the Masonic Hall on Saturday night, when he knocked out in the third round Alex Wilson, (8.12) a promising lightweight from Kandos...the end came with dramatic suddenness. When the men faced each other Murray crowded his opponent on to the ropes and first sent a straight left to the side of the jaw, with such effect that Wilson was so badly rattled that he dropped his guard. Then Murray sent a beautiful right swing which connected partly on Wilson's jaw, and he dropped like a log face downwards to be counted out...Murray displayed cat like agility and though perhaps not as clever as his older brother showed that he carried a punch in either hand. With such qualities young Murray should no doubt meet much cleverer boxers, and will certainly beat more than will beat him. (16 July 1927)

Doolan Murray's reputation grew as his family continued to excel at sport. The *Cowra Guardian* (hereafter *Guardian*) of 23 January 1945 noted Doolan Murray's special place in local boxing. The article recalled the 'thrilling battles and deeds of Doolan Murray', which were 'still fresh in the memories of Cowra fight followers'. By that time Doolan had been training promising local fighters for fifteen years and many of the prominent boxers to emerge from the local fight scene counted him as an early mentor. The *Guardian* reported on 29 October 1943: 'Viney is the son of Doolan Murray, former well-known professional fighter'. In the *Guardian* of 23 January 1945 he was '[t]he famous Doolan Murray'. In a later description he was '[t]hat grand old Cowra fighter' (in Marriott 1988: 286).

The reasons Doolan Murray and his brothers and son were represented in this unique way could be related to a development of the discourse on Aborigines. The idea of Indigenous athletes as role models and examples of what can be achieved despite disadvantage developed later.[3] The stereotype that Aborigines were just not capable of reaching the standards set by white society was not reflected in the emergence of high-profile achievers such as the Murray brothers. Without an alternative way of explaining their achievements, it may have been easier for white commentators to ignore or deny their Aboriginality. In that way, the status quo was maintained and racial groups were kept in their expected place. It may also be that the representations of the Murray athletes were context dependant. At the time when they were succeeding in sport it may have been accepted that Aborigines could excel at boxing as opposed to other sports. This line of argument is supported by the stereotypical representations of the Erambie Allblacks who were the first rugby league team known to be made up entirely of Australian Aborigines to challenge white teams.

The Black Prince: Jim Murray

The changing nature of the representations of the Murray family is illustrated in the way Doolan's son, Harry James 'Jim' Murray, was discussed in local newspapers. As a developing athlete, Jim was claimed as a 'Cowra' athlete and, like his father and uncles before him he was 'Jim the athlete' and not 'Jim the Aborigine'. However, when he began to challenge the treatment of Aborigines in the town a subtle shift in the way he was represented occurred and his race was included in the stories about him as I discuss below.

At the southern end of Erambie mission, 'over the back', Doolan Murray and the men of the mission had built a sports field that included a running track where the community's competitive sprinters trained. Jim told the following story about his introduction to competitive running:

> I often talk about this. Up there at the mission where the road is now, they built a foot-running track along there. Because they had them houses and the line [railway track] and in between them they put, they built a foot-running track. They went and got an old hoop iron with the sulky with it and dragged that around and levelled it all out and they made this track. Poor old Lochie Ingram, Nino [Williams], Arthur [Williams], and the other brother, Peter [Williams]. Poor old Victor Carroll, Vic Simpson. Anyway, I was still going to school, see, and I used to come home from school and they'd be there every night.

Chapter 7

Telling Australian Stories

> Anthony Mundine's a natural: fluid, flashy,
> all speed, explosive power and grace. His
> main advantage will be his ability to stay out
> of Green's way and disable him with rapid
> incursions. His disadvantages will be mental.
> He's yet to prove his mind can't be overcome.
> Is there another way at all of seeing this?
> (Drane 2006: 85)

> Group X always needs group Y to buff its own
> sense of superiority. (Shields 1999: 145)

Aborigines are athletic. The images and words presented in the electronic and print media make this point clear. In the twenty-first century the opportunities for non-Indigenous Australians to learn about Indigenous Australians have increased. We are less likely to be found predominately on missions and reserves, many of us are university educated and we are employed in a variety of professions. Indigenous histories and cultures are taught in schools. Yet even with these changes the country's sporting stadia remain the most visible arenas for Aborigines. Our athletes appear in various media on a daily basis. The result is that the way these athletes are portrayed often embodies a large proportion of what is known about Indigenous Australians. Historically, these depictions have been used to differentiate between black and white Australians. Current portrayals of Indigenous athletes maintain these differences.

Generalising from the case study approach I have used can be difficult. In fact, one of my criticisms of the body of literature on Aborigines in sport is that generalisations about the pervasive nature of racism are forced onto all of the sporting experiences of Aborigines. This, in turn, has led to the limited nature of resulting narratives, so it is my hope that this case study of Erambie mission might produce new ways of looking at Aborigines in sport. Taking ideas from a number of sources, a framework was formed with which to analyse and explain the wide variety of data. Providing frameworks for further study is an outcome that is preferable to generalising about Aborigines as a homogenous group based on this one case. Nevertheless, as I have said earlier, the discursive themes identified in the historical descriptions of Wiradjuri Aborigines persist in contemporary representations of Indigenous athletes. This continuity is demonstrated in examples from print and electronic media that highlight the continuation of the themes in representations about race.

Natural athletes

Where Indigenous athletes are described solely in physical terms, examples of valued character traits such as dependability, intellectual capacity and application are omitted. Using football to reinforce differences between black and white people is common. In fact, it could be considered a sacred Australian sporting story.

In the acclaimed 2002 feature film *Australian rules*, the 'difference' of Aborigines is again evident. In this story of a small Australian community, told through the local football team, Gary 'Blacky' Black (a white teenager played by Nathan Phillips) is depicted as partly heroic for his relationship with the otherwise 'tolerated' mission community. The other central character is Dumby Red (played by Luke Carroll, the great-grandson of Erambie Allblacks player, Stanley Carroll), the athletic and uncoachable black star of the team. The ability of the black players is introduced at the very beginning of the film when the narrator, Blacky, tells the viewer, 'half our team is Aboriginal, boys from the mission. Without them we wouldn't be in the grand final. Without them we wouldn't even have a team'. The story also shows the inevitable racism as it pervades the everyday lives of the people in the town, both black and white. Aborigines are shown being served in their own segregated area of the local pub and white characters continually make racist remarks about the moral character and athletic ability of the 'blacks'. We hear one conversation in which a white coach tells Blacky's father he does not like the company his son keeps (Dumby), while another says, 'geez the little black prick can play footy though, hey'.

The athletic ability of the black players is continually remarked upon as is their difference in moral character. When the coach (played by Kevin Harrington) is preparing his team for the grand final he asks Dumby to 'make sure your blokes don't go walkabout before the game'. In another pre-game scene one of the Indigenous players is arrested at training. We find out why when the coach addresses the team about the incident: 'Carol Cockatoo ain't gonna be playin Sat'dy. Now as youse probably know there's been a few places knocked-off lately, the servo...the pub. Now I'm not pointing the finger at anybody but apparently, apparently Carol was involved.'

The film also touches on differences in meaning attached to games, albeit in a stereotypical way, in two grand-final day scenes. The first comes when the mission players inevitably turn up late, seemingly oblivious to the importance of the match. This scene continues the attack on the stereotype of black athletes going walkabout. It is at least questionable whether the level of satire in this scene is sufficient to challenge the stereotype. In this case, the mission players' cavalier attitude to time-keeping reinforces the stereotype as the viewer may take the scene on face value as an example of the walkabout stereotype. The second scene, during the match itself, shows Dumby — brilliant, athletic and again uncoachable — as he goes against the coach's instructions not to 'muck around on them bloody flanks, no more finessing'. Dumby takes a brilliant mark displaying his athletic ability yet again, before passing up an easy goal to pass to another player from the mission. At the after-match celebration Blacky asks Dumby why he did this.

> Blacky: Did he call for it?
> Dumby: No.
> Blacky: Well why?
> Dumby: Dunno. Well Kicker hardly had a touch all day. Well Kicker's me cus [cousin], you know, I didn't wanna see him shamed like that.
> Blacky: Jesus Dumby, you blackfellas.

Even Blacky, who spends most of his time with the mission boys, cannot understand the mission way of playing the game.

The Erambie football team's story inevitably included repeated examples of the alleged character flaws of the Wiradjuri people. Over eighty years on, the way this story is told has changed little. The story of the athletically gifted Aborigines remains linked to the story of moral inferiority. In this sense, Fanon's arguments are evident, as the identity of Aborigines continues to be controlled by outsiders. As I noted earlier, the markers of difference remain and the message is clear: the Aborigine is athletic *and* he is inferior. The evidence for this comes in the movie when racism is used to explain the main black character committing a crime. Fanon's ideas about the use of language to control colonised people are still evident here. In this version the Aborigine remains inferior, although it may no longer be his fault.

These portrayals are important precisely because they are so common. The film tells a familiar story about racism placing continual obstacles in the way of the black community and its football players. In the end, racism forces Dumby to commit a crime when he realises he would only ever be a black. His death during a robbery and cover-up was the last example of the pervasive nature of racism, which not even natural sporting ability can overcome. The stories that Erambie people tell illustrate how, even when it appears to be at its most debilitating, racism does not necessarily tell the whole story. For Erambie Wiradjuri, cultural practices continued and in many cases racist practices did not result in the complete shutdown or breakdown of daily life for the Wiradjuri of the area. Although this narrative does have a place in the stories of Aborigines in sport, it is not and nor should it become the whole story.

Heroic possibilities

The 'heroic possibilities' of the grievance narrative restrict historical accounts about black athletes. The language of inferiority that is used to tell a story about champion Australian jockey Darby McCarthy has an underlying message that re-occurs in the stories of many of the Indigenous Australian athletes. This uniformity very effectively highlights the nature and extent of racism faced by many Indigenous Australians. However, constant focus on the negative aspects coupled with the supposed 'black magic' creates the impression that there is little more to tell in the Indigenous sporting experiences other than racism and natural ability. In fact, the Indigenous athlete as representative of victimisation has become one of the 'sacred' stories of sport. The transition in thought that emerges through a more nuanced engagement with an Indigenous community's storytelling tradition offers an alternative framework for understanding the performances of Indigenous athletes.

As an example, take the 2006 Australian super fight that pitted Koori boxer Anthony Mundine against Anglo-Australian Danny Green. According to Lalor's article, 'New epic: Mundine v Green draws knockout crowd', the fight generated enormous media interest and broke many attendance and viewing records in Australian boxing (*Australian* 18 May 2006). Two overriding ideas emerged from the media coverage of this event. First, the physical and moral differences between white and black Australians were reinforced: most experts agreed that Anthony Mundine was far superior in athletic ability whereas Green possessed the courage and moral strength. Second, the story of Indigenous victimisation and loss was used to explain Mundine's triumph.

In the lead-up to the fight the relative strengths of the boxers were discussed in the print media. Peter Kogoy of the *Herald Sun* on 13 May 2006 included a number of 'expert' quotes that highlighted the physical attributes of Anthony Mundine. Respected Australian trainer Johnny Lewis is quoted as saying that he believed Mundine's speed would be the decisive difference between the fighters, while former world champion Jeff Fenech considered speed was Mundine's one advantage: 'If there's one thing that Mundine's got on Green, it's speed, but I don't believe he knows how to use his speed properly.' According to Graham Anderson in the *Sydney Morning Herald* of 12 May 2006, German trainer Ulli Wegner said that Mundine has 'got all the natural ability in the world, he's the greatest natural talent that I've ever come across'. In short, 'expert' opinion firmly established Mundine's natural physical ability.

Descriptions of Mundine's natural physical talents were contrasted with Green's supposed advantages in character. Terms such as 'fine young man' and 'quality men like Green' are used in Anderson's article to emphasise the white boxer's character over his physical abilities (12 May 2006). The difference between the two boxers was further reinforced by Wegner: 'Mundine's got the most natural talent, the sheer athleticism and speed. Green's the robust, hard-nosed destroyer.' Mundine, the Aborigine, is the natural athlete not capable of even understanding his own natural gifts, whereas the apparently less athletic

Green demonstrates all that is lacking in the Aborigine: moral character and willpower. If people who are considered knowledgeable say that we are natural athletes who are mentally and morally deficient, it is not difficult to imagine how it might reinforce this view of Aborigines in the wider community, in the same way as the mission managers' descriptions of fights on Erambie may have influenced how Aborigines were seen by outsiders.

Following Mundine's convincing win, the fighters continued to be described according to the discursive themes identified earlier. Mundine was denied credit for all but his physical skills. In an online article for *ABC Sport Online*: 'Man takes out machine', Stuart Watt told his readers, '[t]he Western Australian's [Green] courage was there for all to see, but Mundine was giving him a pasting' (18 May 2006). Mundine's victory was attributed to his superior speed and mobility rather than courage or astute tactical abilities.

Robert Drane's article also employed the stereotypical descriptions of the black and white athletes of his peers. Drane, though, appeared to suggest that the stereotypical language used is appropriate (2006). Echoing Tatz's argument that the data alone overwhelmingly tells the story, he claimed that only one straight-line story is to be told. 'Anthony Mundine's a natural: fluid, flashy, all speed, explosive power and grace…his disadvantage will be mental. He's yet to prove his mind can't be overcome' (85). When he described Green, Drane focused on his supposed mental and moral advantages. Green was continually portrayed as a man to be feared because of his mental and moral strength while Mundine's confidence could only be explained as false bravado. Even past displays of courage from Mundine were qualified as being '[c]ourage that certain opponents strip away quickly'. Despite winning a world title and continuing with a subsequent defence while injured, Mundine was 'yet to demonstrate a stomach for a crisis', whereas Green was 'resolute' and 'determined'. Go back eighty years to the descriptions of Erambie's athletes (with the notable exception of Doolan Murray) and it is apparent that little has changed in the way Aborigines are written about.

Drane chose to describe the fight as a story about deficit. Although Mundine himself did not grow up in a 'squalid' mission or reserve community, he is often linked by the media to this perception of Indigenous communities (Mundine does little to distance himself from this). This is done by emphasising his links to such places either through his father's background or his own visits to various communities. In this type of portrayal the positives of Indigenous physical culture are buried for our own good. Even Indigenous writers often focus on the negatives within their community rather than emphasise the positives. You get a sense that we cannot celebrate our own sporting culture for fear of losing ground in the battle over identity and being blamed for our own victim status. Drane claimed as much when he wrote that Mundine especially represents 'every Aboriginal who never had a chance' and that Mundine's win was a victory for poor blackfellas.

In his account of the action on fight night, Drane continued to deny Mundine all but his physical superiority over the white fighter. Green, although obviously beaten, is 'a brave loser', Mundine is part of an 'inevitable tide' not unlike the way countless black boxers before him have been described. Green, on the other hand, portrayed all of the treasured attributes a white man should posses when he 'nailed every question in the hardest test of knowledge he'd ever known'.

On its own, the description of Mundine as physically rather than morally and intellectually sound may be simply an apt description based on one person's views. It could also stem from Mundine's supposed unpopularity or the personal bias of an individual author. However, viewing the articles within the context of historical accounts and the discursive themes I discuss in this book suggests race as a factor in this consistent denial of all but physical abilities. These narratives reinforce and refine stereotypes. The language that indicates this difference, such as the Jacky vernacular, and the overtly racist terms such as 'coon' and 'abo' have been consigned to the past. However, the continued portrayal of black and white athletes along these established racial lines reinforces the idea that race and certain physical and intellectual differences are invariably linked.

As an example, Cashill offered the following critique of a portrayal by noted American author, Joyce Carol Oates, of Muhammad Ali as a hero of the resistance to racism:

> [R]ejecting any number of alternative ways to introduce Ali...[Oates] could have informed the reader that he was the much-loved offspring to two devoted parents...which may explain his confidence. He had a skilled muralist for a father, a mathematician for an uncle, and a math teacher for an aunt, which may account for his creativity and

instinctive smarts. As for his drive, that likely derived from his status as the first child in an ambitious African-American household...Oates chooses instead to introduce Ali the way Malcolm X might have, not as an American, but as a victim of America, the grandson of a slave. (Cashill 2006: 4)

An example of how the grievance narrative is often used in Australian writing about Aborigines in sport comes from Robert Drane's 2006 article discussed above. In it, Anthony Mundine was framed according to a discourse of deficit and victimhood rather than his social reality. Like Ali, Mundine's success could easily be the story of the middle-class son of a champion athlete who lived a life with many advantages provided by two loving parents (that is, he was not from an overcrowded and impoverished home), and who was exposed to top-class training and coaching from an early age. Instead, Drane framed Mundine's story in line with expectations of the way Indigenous athletes should be seen. Anything else, I believe, runs the risk of minimising the pervasive effects of racism and challenging the victim label. Drane wrote that Mundine has 'come to represent every Aboriginal, especially every Aboriginal who never had a chance'. Conforming with the grievance narrative, Drane told us that Mundine 'won for his tribes-people who had died at the hands of white neglect'. Suggesting that the stereotypical language he used was appropriate, Drane asked, '[i]s there another way of seeing' fights between black and white boxers, before answering his own question that there was not. Conforming to such an identity, Mundine himself embraces being associated with the grievance narrative as part of his approach to self and event promotion and to confronting racism in society. For example, Mundine planned to use his profile in sport to 'send our plight to the world' (in Falcous & Silk 2006: 325).

Stories to tell

There is a link between common ways that stories are told and the assumption of loss that invariably produces deficit narratives about Indigenous people's sporting experiences. Contradictions have emerged in the way these experiences have been viewed, with stories from within the Erambie community generally suggesting a link between pre-contact Wiradjuri culture and mission culture. Using an approach that includes these contrasting understandings and ways of knowing, there is the possibility of continuity or retention of cultural practices where loss is often expected. Including Indigenous understandings and meanings of sport allows for continuity of aspects of our cultures to at least be considered.

The approaches used to examine and represent Indigenous cultures have led many Wiradjuri people to argue that outsiders cannot produce valid examinations of our communities. I do not agree with this argument. However, this does not alter my position that understanding of the meanings a community attaches to sports, events and individuals can only come from within the community itself. This means reconsidering the reliance on documentary sources and working with the oral history traditions of Indigenous communities and undertaking prolonged observations. This approach is more likely to uncover the meanings that Indigenous people attach to valued cultural practices. The idea that all change should be considered as a loss needs to be altered to consider what our communities have gained. By not approaching every Indigenous sporting story with the assumption of victimhood, a greater variety of experiences emerges. Aborigines do have a life outside white intervention and it does involve some social and cultural practices that have survived and evolved after colonisation by whites. As it stands, continuity can never be identified within our communities as long as the approaches to telling Indigenous people's stories are based on the assumption of loss.

Aborigines in sport

Aborigines are different. The way Aborigines are written about in the sports discourse introduces and reinforces differences associated with race. Indigenous voices have historically been omitted from the sports discourse. In this respect, there is an identifiable continuity in the way Aborigines are presented in the context of sport. Stemming from the period of colonisation and enduring through post-colonial times, these representations can be explained using theories about control of indigenous identities. There is enough repetition to suggest that the theories utilised have 'travelled' well from their origins in colonial studies. The explanations by Fanon and Memmi (1957/2003) of the coloniser's use of language to establish inferiority fitted with the way Erambie Aborigines were written about by white people. The approaches used to analyse historical events were reinforcing difference, albeit with a shift in focus. As a result, Aborigines have been given a new identity, or at least a newer version of an old identity, as victims. This supports Hall's description of race being a floating signifier which maintains racial hierarchies. Approaching Indigenous people's sporting experiences with the assumption of inferiority reduces the variety of narratives told about the topic. What this does in effect is to reinforce the difference, and more importantly, the notion of the inferiority of Aborigines.

Aborigines are victims. To be the victimised or the unfortunate other requires some evidence or examples, and the reported sporting success of Indigenous athletes supplies this evidence. Aborigines, it has been written, excel at sports because colonisation has made our communities such bad places that we are desperate to escape them. Continued racism makes sport the only practical avenue by which we can escape. The evidence used to support this idea of victimhood places our communities in an inferior position to non-Indigenous communities. When Indigenous sporting stories are repeatedly told using a limited number of discursive themes the inferiority of our communities is reinforced. Therefore, Aborigines allegedly excel at sport because our communities and culture are now inferior to white society. The dominance of this narrative supports Foucault's ideas about power and the production of knowledge. Aborigines continue to be victims because people say we are.

Aborigines continue our traditions. Erambie's Wiradjuri community retains aspects of our culture through sport. The Erambie community had a life independent of white intrusions. This is significant for a contemporary Wiradjuri community that was supposed to be removed from the 'authentic' culture of its ancestors. It is also of significance when explanations of Indigenous people's achievements and experiences in sport are offered because 'internal' factors such as continuity of sporting culture should be considered. As difficult as it may be to do, researchers should more often consider the possibility that our communities have experiences and ways of being that are independent of mainstream society.

Questions of continuity are linked to interpretation. Even when differences observed in the mission culture of Erambie were also identified in pre-contact Wiradjuri cultures, it can be difficult to prove that this is due to continuity. The complexity of 'knowing' these observable differences means they are open to interpretation. Stories that portray loss and deficit within Indigenous communities represent only limited experiences. Erambie people continue to live Wiradjuri culture. The storytelling that drives the community's oral history tradition is an example of this cultural continuity. However, this belief is contrasted with the idea that, for whatever reason, contemporary Wiradjuri culture, including sport and physical activity, is not sufficiently connected to the past to be termed continuity.

There is an identifiable straight-line story being told about Indigenous peoples' experiences in sport. However, storytellers such as those from Erambie Mission rarely tell such narrowly focused histories. They are not afraid to leave the straight line to tell stories that make us human. Moving away from the straight line should be a future focus of research in this area.

Watching the Mundine–Green fight within my own community gave me an insight into what it might have been like to watch a Doolan Murray fight or an Erambie Allblacks match and read the subsequent newspaper descriptions. For the Kooris who I watched this fight with, Mundine's victory was explained by his Aboriginality just as it had been for the non-Indigenous journalists who covered the fight. However, the comments made by those I watched the fight with indicated that he did not represent a victimised group of people, nor did he represent a race that is athletically gifted and lacking in mental abilities and courage. Instead, they discuss Anthony Mundine as symbolic of cultures that still develop clever people. For the people who I watched this fight with, Mundine had mental as well as physical advantages over his opponent that are a gift of his race. As the Storyteller would say, he was just too clever.

Returning to the question that opened this chapter and informs much of what this book is about — whether there are other ways to see the success and abilities of Indigenous athletes. A change of approach will uncover other ways of seeing Indigenous communities and the athletes who represent them. Perhaps Drane should have asked this question in more than a rhetorical sense. There are other ways to identify and write stories about Indigenous people.

There is a dimension to life within Indigenous communities that the rest of Australia does not see enough of, if they see it at all. This other dimension adds to the vibrant iconic images, the inspiring creativity of Indigenous dance and artwork. It is the stories that are told through a beautiful oral history tradition that are the most important part of our culture. If we are to survive beyond the physical sense, as Wiradjuri, as Koori, as Indigenous people, we need our stories because they tell us who we are.

Notes

Chapter 1

1. See for example Sutton 2009; Pearson 2000, 2007, 2009; Maddison 2009.

2. Tatz continued to make the argument that sport mirrors racism in society (1995a, 1995b). More examples of accumulation of this argument can be seen in Corris 1979; Cashman 1995; Hallinan 1991; Hallinan, Eddleman and Oslim 1991; Vamplew and Stoddart 1994; Trengrove 1996; Hallinan, Bruce and Coram 1999; Coram 1999; Hartley 2002; Mallett 2002.

Chapter 2

1. The Aborigines Protection Board func-tioned from about 1883 to 1940, when its name was changed to Aborigines Welfare Board (http://www.records.nsw.gov.au/state-archives/guides-and-finding-aids/archives-in-brief/archives-in-brief-42).

2. See Peter Read's (1984b) and Peter Rimas-Kabaila's (1996) collections of oral histories from Erambie to read other people's fond memories of growing up at Erambie.

Chapter 3

1. Throughout this chapter I have written 'Allblacks' as a single word. This is in contrast to the two words 'All Blacks' which is how the team was represented in the district newspapers. The usage I have employed represents the way the team is known within the community.

Chapter 4

1. Historian Henry Reynolds has detailed the history and intention of making judgments regarding the caste of people all over the world. In his 2005 book, *Nowhere people*, Reynolds writes that the terms used to describe people with a mixture of racial ancestry went beyond the simply descriptive: they reflected a racial hierarchy. Reynolds also argued that it was generally accepted that people of mixed race were morally and physically defective, unpredictable, unstable and degenerate. Foster appears to be reinforcing this point in his speech.

Chapter 5

1. NSW Death Certificate 1909/9015 lists Sam Murray's age at 35 in 1909 meaning he was born in 1874. Harry Murray was born two years before (NSW Death Certificate 1938/22224).

2. NSW Death Certificate 1909/9015.

3. I am aware that there are instances, such as those presented in this book, where black athletes such as Joe Louis are retrospec-tively described as being role models for other black people. However, it is not clear that this concept was prevalent during their careers.

4. Copies of reports produced by the Aborigines Protection Board and the Aborigines Welfare Board are common within the community. Many people collect them during family history research relating to stolen wages and Native Title claims. They are often shared and read by senior men and women during conversations. People often discuss claims made in the reports about people and the community in general, and as such they have become part of the oral history of the community.

Bibliography

Adair, D 2006, 'Shooting the messenger: Australian history's warmongers', *Sporting Traditions*, vol. 22, no. 2, pp. 49–69.

Adair, D & Vamplew, W 1997, *Sport in Australian history*, Oxford University Press, Melbourne.

Allport G 1954, *The nature of prejudice*, Addison-Wesley, Cambridge.

Anderson, W 2002, *The cultivation of whiteness: Science, health and racial destiny in Australia*, Melbourne University Press.

Angelou M 1984, *I know why a caged bird sings*, Virago Press, London.

Attwood, B & Markus, A 2007, *The 1967 referendum: Race, power and the Australian constitution*, Aboriginal Studies Press, Canberra.

Bachelor, D 1948, *British boxing*, Collins, London.

Bale, J & Sang, J 1996, *Kenyan running: Movement culture, geography and global change*, Frank Cass, London.

Bamblett, L 2011, 'Straight-line stories: Representations and Indigenous Australian identities in sports discourse', *Australian Aboriginal Studies*, no. 2, pp. 5–20.

Bamblett, M 1995, 'The Maryula dog', in M Bamblett, J Ingram, G Carroll, D Holmes, A Armstrong-Holmes & T Williams, *Memories of the past*, Cowra TAFE, unpaginated.

Barthes, R 1957/1972, *Mythologies*, Hill & Wang, New York.

Bass, A (ed.) 2005, *In the game: Race, identity, and sports in the twentieth century*, Palgrave Macmillan, New York.

Beckett, J 1977, in A Elkin, *Aboriginal men of high degree* (2nd edn), University of Queensland Press, St Lucia.

Behrendt, L 2001, 'Cathy Freeman and the politics of sport', *Journal of Australian Indigenous Issues*, vol. 4, no. 1, pp. 27–9.

Bennett, G 1834/1967, *Wanderings in New South Wales, Batavia, Pedir Coast, Singapore and China: Being the journal of a naturalist in those countries during 1832, 1833 and 1834*, vol. 1, (facsimile edn), Libraries Board of South Australia, Adelaide.

Berndt, R 1947, 'Wuradjeri magic and "clever men"', *Oceania*, vol. 17, pp. 327–65.

Beveridge, P 1899, 'Of the Aborigines inhabiting the great lacustrine and riverine depression of the lower Murrumbidgee, lower Lachlan, and lower Darling', *Journal and Proceedings of the Royal Society of New South Wales*, vol. 17, pp. 19–74.

Bloom, J 2000, *To show what an Indian can do: sports at Native American boarding schools*, University of Minnesota Press, Minneapolis.

Booth, D & Tatz, C 2000, *One-eyed: A view of Australian sport*, Allen & Unwin, St Leonards.

Brailsford, D 1988, *Bareknuckles: A social history of prizefighting*, Lutterworth Press, Cambridge.

Broome, R 1980, 'Professional Aboriginal boxers in eastern Australia 1930–1979', *Aboriginal History*, vol. 4, no. 1, pp. 49–72.

—— 1996, 'Theatres of power: Tent boxing circa 1910–1970', *Aboriginal History*, vol. 20, pp. 1–23.

—— 2005, *Aboriginal Victorians: A history since 1800*, Allen & Unwin, Crows Nest.

Calloway, L 2004 *Darby McCarthy: Against all odds*, Melbourne Books, Melbourne.

Cashill, J 2006, *Sucker punch: The hard left hook that dazed Ali and killed King's dream*, Nelson Current, Nashville.

Cashman, R 1995, *Paradise of sport: The rise of organized sport in Australia*, Oxford University Press, South Melbourne.

Clayton, I & Barlow, A 1997, *Wiradjuri of the rivers and plains*, Heinemann Library, Port Melbourne.

Coe, M 1989, *Windradyne: A Wiradjuri Koorie*, Aboriginal Studies Press, Canberra.

Coram, S 1999, *Reclaiming Aboriginal identity through Australian rules football: A legacy of the 'stolen generation'*, viewed 16 June 2006, <http://fulltext.ausport.gov.au/fulltext/1999/nsw/p159-164.asp>.

—— 2001, 'The burden of Australian Indigenous athletes: Teaching non-Indigenes about racism', in M Nakata (ed.), *Indigenous people, racism and the United Nations*, Common Ground Publishing, Altona, pp. 89–100.

Corris, P 1979, *Lords of the ring: A history of prize-fighting in Australia*, Cassell Australia, North Ryde.

Craze, B & Marriott, J 1988, 'The Aborigines', in J Marriott (ed.), *Cowra on the Lachlan*, Cowra Shire Council, pp. 1–8.

Danielson, M 1997, *Home team: Professional sports and the American metropolis*, Princeton University Press, Princeton.

Douglas, M 1966/2002, *Purity and danger: An analysis of concepts of pollution and taboo*, Routledge, London.

Drane, R 2006, 'The fight', *Inside Sport*, no. 175, July, pp. 84–91.

Eagleton, T 2000, *The idea of culture*, Blackwell, Oxford.

Elkin, A 1977, *Aboriginal men of high degree* (2nd edn), University of Queensland Press, St Lucia.

Erenberg, L 2006, *The greatest fight of our generation: Louis vs. Schmeling*, Oxford University Press, New York.

Falcous, M & Silk, M 2006, 'Global regimes, local agendas: Sport, resistance and the mediation of dissent', *International Review for the Sociology of Sport*, vol. 41, no. 3, pp. 317–38.

Fanon, F 1952/1970, *Black skin white mask*, Granada Publishing, London.

—— 1967, *The wretched of the earth*, Penguin Books, London.

Flood, J 1980, *The moth hunters: Aboriginal pre-history of the Australian alps*, Australian Institute of Aboriginal Studies, Canberra.

Folster, W & Weathersten, PW 1988, *W. Folster's articles: the writings of William (Bill) Folster*, P Weathersten, Orange.

Foucault, M 1966/2002, *The order of things: An archaeology of the human sciences*, Routledge Classics, London.

Gammage, B 1986, *Narrandera Shire*, Narrandera Shire Council, Narrandera.

Gardiner, G 1997, 'Racial abuse and football: The Australian Football League's racial vilification rule in review', *Sporting Traditions*, vol. 14, no.1, pp. 3–25.

—— 2003, 'Black bodies — white codes: Indigenous footballers, racism and the Australian Football League's racial and religious vilification code', in J Bale & M Cronin (eds), *Sport and*

Postcolonialism, Berg, Oxford, pp. 29–44.

Gems, G 1999, 'A response to "Playing Indian"', *American Indian Culture and Research Journal*, vol. 23, no. 2, pp. 133–5.

Gilbert, K 1973/2002, *Because a white man'll never do it*, Angus & Robertson Classics, Pymble.

Godwell, D 1997, 'Aboriginality and rugby league in Australia: An exploratory study of identity construction and professional sport', unpublished masters thesis, University of Windsor, Canada.

—— 2000, 'Playing the game: Is sport as good for race relations as we'd like to think?', *Australian Aboriginal Studies*, vol. 1, no. 2, pp. 12–19.

Gorman, S 2008, 'Blak magik: Indigenous identity and the media in the 1980s', in P Burke & J Senyard (eds), *Behind the play: football in Australia*, Maribyrnong Press, Hawthorn, pp. 189–99.

—— 2011, *Legends: The AFL Indigenous team of the century*, Aboriginal Studies Press, Canberra.

Gorringe, S, Ross, J & Fforde, C 2011, 'Will the real Aborigine please stand up': Strategies for breaking the stereotypes and changing the conversation, Research Discussion Paper no. 28, Australian Institute of Aboriginal and Torres Strait Islander Studies, Canberra.

Gratton, C & Jones, I 2004, *Research methods for sports studies*, Routledge, London.

Haagen C 1994, *Bush toys: Aboriginal children at play*, Aboriginal Studies Press, Canberra.

Hall, R 1998, *Black armband days: Truth from the dark side of Australia's past*, Random House, Sydney.

Hall, S 1997a, *Representation: Cultural representations and signifying practices*, Sage, London.

—— 1997b, *Race: The floating signifier*, speech presented at Goldsmiths College, London, England [transcript], viewed 27 May 2011, <http://www.mediaed.org/assets/products/407/transcript_407.pdf>.

Hallinan, C 1991, 'Aborigines and positional segregation in Australian rugby league', *International Review for the Sociology of Sport*, no. 26, pp. 69–81.

Hallinan, C, Bruce, T & Coram, S 1999, 'Up front and beyond the centre line: Australian Aborigines in elite Australian rules football', *International Review for the Sociology of Sport*, vol. 34, no. 4, pp. 369–83.

Hallinan, C, Eddleman, K & Oslim, J 1991, 'Racial segregation by playing position in elite Australian basketball', *Australian Journal of Science and Medicine in Sport*, vol. 23, no. 4, pp. 111–14.

Hamilton, D (ed.) 1981, *Cognitive processes in stereotyping and intergroup behaviours*, Erlbaum, Hillsdale.

Hamilton, D & Sherman, S 1989, 'Illusory correlation: Implications for stereotype theory and research', in D Bar-Tal, C Graumann, A Kruglanski & W Stroebe (eds), *Stereotyping and prejudice: Changing concepts*, Springer-Verlag, London, pp. 59–82.

Hardy, S 1996, 'Continuity and long residuals', *Proceedings and Newsletter*, North American Society for Sport History, p. 78.

BIBLIOGRAPHY

Harper, D 2004, 'Photography as social science', in U Flick, E v Kordorff & I Steinke, *A companion to qualitative research*, Sage, London, pp. 231–6.

Harris, B 1984, *Ella, Ella, Ella*, Little Hills Press, Crows Nest.

—— 1989, *The proud champions: Australia's Aboriginal sporting heroes*, Little Hills Press, Crows Nest.

Hartley, J 2002, 'Black, white…and red? The Redfern All Blacks Rugby League Club in the early 1960s', *Labour History*, no. 83, pp. 149–72.

Hay, R 2006, 'Approaches to sports history: Theory and practice', *Sporting Traditions*, vol. 22, no. 2, pp. 77–8.

Heads, I 1992, *True blue: The story of the New South Wales Rugby League*, Iron Bark Press, Randwick.

Hewstone, M & Browne, R (eds) 1986, *Contact and conflict in intergroup encounters*, Blackwell, Oxford.

Hinton, P 2000, *Stereotypes, cognition, and culture*, Psychology Press, Hove.

Hoberman, J 1997, *Darwin's athletes: How sport has damaged black America and preserved the myth of race*, Houghton Mifflin, Boston.

Holt R 1989, *Sport and the British: A modern history*, Oxford University Press, Oxford.

Horner, J 1994, *Bill Ferguson: Fighter for Aboriginal freedom*, Author, Dickson.

Howitt, A 1996, *The native tribes of south-eastern Australia*, Aboriginal Studies Press, Canberra.

Ingamells, R 1951, *The great south land: An epic poem*, Georgion House, Melbourne.

Ingram S 2003, *Stepping out and speakin' up*, Older Women's Network NSW, Millers Point.

Jhally, S 1996, *Race: The Floating Signifier*, DVD, Media Education Foundation, Northampton.

Judd, B 2005, 'Joe Johnson: The "first" Aborigine in the VFL?', *Journal of Australian Indigenous Issues*, vol. 8, no. 2, pp. 31–8.

Judd, B & Hallinan, C 2008, 'Hoop dreams: Essentialised constructs', *Journal of Australian Indigenous Issues*, vol. 11, no. 4, pp. 17–24.

Kane, J 1997, 'Racialism and democracy: The legacy of White Australia', in G Stokes (ed.), *The politics of identity in Australia*, Cambridge University Press, Cambridge, pp. 117–31.

Keating, P 1994, *Worlds apart: Life on an Aboriginal Mission*, Hale & Iremonger, Sydney.

Kelton, J 1997, 'An overview of the history of Aboriginal occupation in the Lachlan Valley', in J Hildred, Forbes Shire Council & Forbes History Book Committee, *The history of Forbes, New South Wales, Australia*, Forbes Shire Council, Forbes, pp. 14–17.

Langton, M 2011, 'Anthropology, politics and the changing world of Aboriginal Australians', *Anthropological Forum*, vol. 21, no. 1, pp. 1–22.

Lansdown, H & Spillius, A (eds) 1990, *Saturday's boys: The football experience*, Willow Books, London.

Lazarus, M & Goldman, P 2002, *Australian Rules*, video recording, Palace Entertainment, Moore Park.

Leab, D 1975, *From Sambo to Superspade: The black experience in motion pictures*, Houghton Mifflin, Boston.

Lee, Y, Jussim, L & McCauley C 1995, *Stereotype accuracy: Toward appreciating group differences*, American Psychological Association, Washington.

Macdonald, G 1986, *The Koori way: The dynamics of cultural distinctiveness in settled Australia*, unpublished doctoral dissertation, University of Sydney.

—— 1991, 'A Wiradjuri fight story', in I Keen (ed.), *Being black: Aboriginal cultures in settled Australia*, Aboriginal Studies Press, Canberra.

—— 2001, 'Does "culture" have "history"? Thinking about continuity and change in central New South Wales', *Aboriginal History*, vol. 25, pp. 176-99.

Maddison, S 2009, *Black politics: Inside the complexity of Aboriginal political culture*, Allen & Unwin, Crows Nest.

Maguire, J 1901, 'Buggeen — The evil spirit', *Science of Man*, 22 June, p. 88.

Mallett, A 2002, *The black lords of summer: The story of the 1868 Aboriginal tour of England and beyond*, University of Queensland Press, St Lucia.

Manne, R (ed.), 2003 *Whitewash: On Keith Windshuttle's Fabrication of Aboriginal history*, Black Ink Agenda, Melbourne.

Marqusee, M 1999, *Redemption song: Muhammad Ali and the spirit of the sixties*, Verso, London.

Marriott, J (ed.) 1988, *Cowra on the Lachlan*, Cowra Shire Council, Cowra.

Martin, G 1978, *Episodes of old Canberra*, Australian National University Press, Canberra.

Masters, R 2006, The Tom Brock Lecture 2005, *The great Fibros versus Silvertails wars*, Tom Brock Bequest Committee, Australian Society for Sport History, Sydney.

Maynard, J 2002, *Aboriginal stars of the turf: Jockeys of Australian racing history*, Aboriginal Studies Press, Canberra.

—— 2011, *The Aboriginal soccer tribe: A history of Aboriginal involvement with the world game*, Magabala Books, Broome.

McAdam, C 1995, *Boundary lines: Charlie McAdam and family*, McPhee Gribble, Ringwood.

McCoy, B 2002, 'The hidden culture of Indigenous football', *Overland*, vol. 166, Autumn, pp. 30-4.

—— 2008, *Holding men: Kanyirninpa and the health of Aboriginal men*, Aboriginal Studies Press, Canberra.

McGregor, R 1997, *Imagined destinies: Aboriginal Australians and the doomed race theory, 1880-1939*, Melbourne University Press, Carlton.

McKenna, M 1997, *Different perspectives on black armband history*, Research Paper no. 5, Information and Research Services, Dept. of the Parliamentary Library, Canberra.

McKnight, D 1986, 'Fighting in an Australian Aboriginal supercamp', in D Riches (ed.), *The Anthropology of Violence*, Blackwell, Oxford.

Memmi, A 1957/2003, *The colonizer and the colonized* (3rd edn), Earthscan, London.

Mulvaney D 1967, *Cricket walkabout: The Australian Aboriginal cricketers on tour 1867-8*, Melbourne University Press, Carlton.

Musgrave, S 1926, *The wayback*, Cumberland Argus, Parramatta.

Myler, P 2005, *Ring of hate: Joe Louis vs. Max Schmeling: The fight of the century*, Arcade Publishing, New York.

Nakata, M 2007, *Disciplining the savages: Savaging the disciplines*, Aboriginal Studies Press, Canberra.

Nelson, A 2009, 'Sport, physical activity and urban Indigenous young people', *Australian Aboriginal Studies*, no. 2, pp. 101–11.

Norman, H 2006, 'A modern day corroboree: Towards a history of the New South Wales Aboriginal rugby league knockout', *Aboriginal History*, no. 30, pp. 169–86.

—— 2009, 'An unwanted corroboree: The politics of the New South Wales Aboriginal rugby league knockout', *Australian Aboriginal Studies*, no. 2, pp. 112–22.

Pearson, N 2000, *Our right to take responsibility*, Noel Pearson and Associates, Cairns.

—— 2007, 'White guilt, victimhood and the quest for a radical centre', *Griffith Review*, no. 16, pp. 13–58.

—— 2009, *Up from the mission: Selected writings*, Black Inc, Collingwood.

Perry, J 2002, *The quick and the dead: Stawell and its race through time*, University of New South Wales Press, Sydney.

Pickering, M 2001, *Stereotyping: The politics of representation*, Palgrave, New York.

Pollard, J 1968, *The Ampol book of Australian sporting records*, Pollard Publishing Co, Sydney.

Read, P 1983, 'A history of the Wiradjuri people of NSW 1883–1969', unpublished doctoral thesis, Australian National University.

—— 1984a, '"Breaking up the camps entirely": The dispersal policy in Wiradjuri country 1909–1929', *Aboriginal History*, vol. 8, no. 4, pp. 45–55.

—— (ed.) 1984b, *Down there with me on the Cowra Mission: An oral history of Erambie Aboriginal Reserve, Cowra, New South Wales*, Permagon Press, Sydney.

—— 1988, *A hundred years war: The Wiradjuri people and the state*, Australian National University Press, Canberra.

Reed, A 1969, *An illustrated encyclopedia of Aboriginal life*, JW Books, Brookvale.

Reynolds, H 2005, *Nowhere people*, Penguin, Camberwell.

Rigney, D 2003, 'Sport, indigenous Australians and invader dreaming: a critique', in J Bale & M Cronin (eds), *Sport and postcolonialism*, Berg, Oxford, pp. 45–56.

Rimas-Kabaila, P 1996, *Wiradjuri places: The Lachlan River basin* (vol. 2), Black Mountain Projects, Jamison.

Ritchie, D 1995, *Doing oral history*, Twayne Publishers, New York.

Ruck, R 1993, *Sandlot seasons: Sport in black Pittsburgh*, University of Illinois Press, Chicago.

Russell, L 2001, *Savage imaginings: Historical and contemporary constructions of Australian Aboriginalities*, Australian Scholarly Publishing, Melbourne.

Sailes G 1998, 'Betting against the odds: An overview of black sports participation', in G Sailes (ed.), *African Americans in sport*, Transaction Publishers, London, pp. 23–5.

Sammons, JT 1994, 'Race and sport', *Journal of Sport History*, vol. 21, no. 3, pp. 203–78.

Sherif, M & Sherif, C 1953, *Groups in harmony and tension*, Harper, New York.

Shields, C, Bishop, R & Mazawi, A 2005, *Pathologising practices: The impact of deficit thinking on education*, Peter Lang, New York.

Shields, D 1999, *Black planet: Facing race during an NBA season*, Three Rivers Press, New York.

Slicaa, H, Thompson, P, Bennett, A & Cross, N 1998, 'Ways of listening', in R Perks & A Thompson (eds), *The oral history reader*, Routledge, London, pp. 114–40.

Smith, S & Sykes, R 1981, *Mum Shirl: An autobiography*, Heinemann, Richmond.

Stokes, G (ed.) 1997, *The politics of identity in Australia*, Cambridge University Press, Melbourne.

Sutton, P 2009, *The politics of suffering: Indigenous Australia and the end of the liberal consensus*, Melbourne University Press.

Tatz, C 1984, 'Race, politics and sport', *Sporting Traditions*, vol. 1, no. 1, pp. 2–36.

—— 1987, *Aborigines in sport*, The Australian Society for Sports History, Bedford Park.

—— 1995a, *Obstacle race: Aborigines in sport*, University of New South Wales Press, Sydney.

—— 1995b, 'Racism and sport in Australia', *Race and Class*, vol. 36, no. 4, pp. 43–54.

Tatz, C & Adair, P 2009, 'Darkness and a little light: Race and sport in Australia', *Australian Aboriginal Studies*, no. 2, pp. 1–14.

Tatz, C & Tatz, P 1996, *Black diamonds: the Aboriginal and Islander sports hall of fame*, Allen & Unwin, St Leonards.

—— 2000, *Black gold: Aborigines and Islander sporting hall of fame*, Aboriginal Studies Press, Canberra.

Taylor, P 1992, *Telling it like it is: A guide to making Aboriginal and Torres Strait Islander history*, Australian Institute of Aboriginal and Torres Strait Islander Studies, Canberra.

Trengrove, A 1996, 'A harder race to run: Colour bar lifts', *The Bulletin*, 19 March, pp. 84–5.

Troy, J 1993, *King plates: A history of Aboriginal gorgets*, Aboriginal Studies Press, Canberra.

Vamplew W & Stoddart, B (eds), 1994 *Sport in Australia: A social history*, Cambridge University Press, Cambridge.

Walker, C 2000, *Buried country: The story of Aboriginal country music*, Pluto Press, Annandale.

Walmsley, K & Kosuth, B 2000, 'Fighting it out in nineteenth-century upper Canada/Canada West: Masculinities in the tavern', *Journal of Sport History*, vol. 27, no. 3, pp. 405–30.

Whimpress, B 1999, *Passport to nowhere: Aborigines in Australian cricket 1850–1939*, Walla Walla Press, Petersham.

—— 2002, 'The first Aboriginal test cricketer', *Journal of the Cricket Society*, vol. 20, no. 4, pp. 5–12.

Williams, R 1993, 'Culture is ordinary', in A Gray & J McGuigan (eds), *Studying culture: An introductory reader*, Edward Arnold, London, pp. 5–14.

Index

INDEX

An 'n' after a page number refers to an endnote.

ABC Sport Online 182
Aboriginal and Torres Strait Islander Commission 20
Aboriginal culture 163–8
  see also Wiradjuri people
Aboriginal men of high degree (Elkin) 127–8
The Aboriginal soccer tribe (Maynard) 30
Aboriginal stars of the turf... (Maynard) 30
Aboriginal Victorians: A history from 1880 (Broome) 153–4
Aborigines in sport
  adoption of rugby 84–5
  during colonial times 128–9
  differing views of 7, 86
  Indigenous perceptions of 26–34, 82–6
  link between sport and music 87–8, 90
  'natural athletes' 26, 178–80
  overview 185–8
  public representations of 15, 17–19, 29, 34–5, 177–8, 180–4
  racism in sport 22–6, 33, 67–8, 70, 73, 89, 153, 177–8, 180
  representation of in newspapers 47, 65–80, 82–3, 86–99, 106–7, 125, 130–3, 135, 153–4, 158–9, 181
  social control through sport 169
  social inclusion 80–6
  stereotypes of 14–15, 19, 68, 75–7, 89–94, 98–9, 179, 182, 184
  Tatz on 16, 22
  traditional Wiradjuri games 50–1, 84–5
  white explanations of black prowess 155–60
  see also Erambie Allblacks
Aborigines in sport (Tatz) 16, 22
Aborigines Protection Board
  appoints white manager 76, 131
  attempts to stop fighting at Erambie 105–9
  forced removal of children by 172
  intrusion into people's lives by 59
  management of Erambie Mission 41, 43, 49, 76, 84, 105
  name change 190n
  petitioned by Cowra residents 74

treatment of the Murrays by 133–4, 155, 157, 159
Aborigines Welfare Board
  attempts to stop fighting at Erambie 108
  forced removal of children by 172
  intrusion into people's lives by 57
  name change 190n
  treatment of the Murrays by 159
Adair, D 23–4, 26, 168
African-Americans 22–3, 129, 157
Agnes (storyteller) 155
alcohol 109, 119
Ali, Muhammad 183–4
Allblacks see Erambie Allblacks
Allport, G 75
The Ampol book of Australian sporting records (Pollard) 19
Anderson, Graham 181
Anderson, Reg 141
Anderson, W 128
Angelou, Maya 156
Australian 181
Australian Association for the Advancement of Science 128
Australian Football League 20
Australian Labor Party 132
Australian rules (film) 178–80
Australian rules football 96–7, 152–3
authenticity 167

Bachelor, D 105
Bale, J 169–70
Bamblett, A 96
Bamblett, James 'Cutter' 66, 94, 155
Bamblett, Mavis 44–5, 47, 51, 53–4, 56–60, 66, 108, 113, 145–6, 155, 172–4
Bamblett, Rebecca 147
Barlow, A 40
Barnard, James 128
Barthes, R 17
Bass, A 70
Baxter, Ern 139–40, 144
Because a white man'll never do it (Gilbert) 19–20
Beckett, Jeremy 127
Beckham, Commissioner 41
Beggeen (evil spirit) 51
Behrendt, Larissa 30
Bennett, Elley 19

INDEX

Berndt, Ronald 126–7
Beveridge, P 50, 84–5
Bicentenary (1988) 20
bidja 128–34, 170, 172
Billy (storyteller) 53
Bingham, Henry 41
binjaling 115–16
birricks 50, 172
Bishop, R 14
'black armband' view of history 23
Blayney 96, 141
Bloom, J 157
Booth, D 70
Bourke's Stadium, Cowra 137, 139
boxing
    career of Claude Murray 148–9
    career of Doolan Murray 66, 135–48, 156–7
    introduction of gloves 118
    Mundine–Green fight 181–4, 187
    portrayal of Muhammad Ali 183–4
    in ritualised fighting 104–5, 117
    Storyteller's career in 3–4
    tent boxing 143
Brailsford, D 105, 118, 120
Brian (storyteller) 44
Briggs, Alex 96
Broome, Richard 20, 25, 33, 153–4
Broughton, Frank 'Bully' 66, 71, 79
Browne, R 75
Brungle Station 42
Budjarn (Wiradjuri clever man) 159
buggenj 51, 172
bugi:nja 126
Bulletin 92–3
bunyips 51–2
burramaldine 58–9

Callaghan (drover) 53
Calloway, Lauren 24–5
Carberry, Harold 96–7
Carcoar Chronicle 78–9
Carroll, Johnno 54
Carroll, Luke 178
Carroll, Robert senior 66
Carroll, Stanley 66–7, 89, 178
Carroll, Victor 150
Cashill, Jack 15, 163, 183–4
Cashman, R 23–4

Charles, John 66
children, forced removal of 56–8, 172
Christianity 104–5
Clark, NC 130
Clayton, Iris 40
'clever' Wiradjuri men 126–7, 146–8, 159
Coe, Agnes 98
Coe, Edie 147
Coe, Isabel 155
Coe, Les 98
Coe, Mary 40, 131
Coe, Paul 98
Coe, Paul 'Callaghan' 66
colonialism, and language 75–6, 93
Commonwealth Games (Brisbane 1982) 20
Condobolin Football Club 88–9
Constable, Mr (manager) 132–3
constructivism 125
continuity, concept of 165–71, 185, 187
Cook, James 53
Cooley Cup 68–9
Cooper, Lynchy 153
Cootamundra Liberal 156–7
Coram, Stella 24
Corris, P 105, 118
Cowan, Alec 137
Cowra 41–2, 57, 87, 137
Cowra Athletic Club 135
Cowra Football Club 153
Cowra Free Press
    on Doolan Murray 134
    on Major Murray 148
    reports on boxing 105, 135–45
    reports on fights at Erambie 107–8
    reports on sprinting 129, 131
    reports on Wiradjuri music performance 55
    representation of Aborigines in 65–9, 71–80, 82–3, 86–9, 91–4, 99, 125, 130–3
Cowra Guardian 149, 153
Cowra Pioneers 66–7, 69–74, 76–7, 82–3, 87, 89, 91, 95
Cowra Rovers 141
Cowra Teachers' Association 107
Crawford, Laurie 34–5, 46
Craze, B 40
cricket 27, 87, 169–70
Cricket walkabout (Mulvaney) 18
Crown Land Commissioners 40–1

cultural continuity 165–71, 185, 187
culture, defined 165
curlew birds 52

dancing 59–60
Danielson, M 80
Darcy, Les 140
Darcy (storyteller) 44, 53
deficit thinking 14, 20, 33–5, 44, 163, 171, 173
discontinuity 166, 168
dispute resolution *see* fights, to resolve disputes
Donaldson, Mr (APB representative) 132
Douglas, Mary 17, 34, 99, 158
Doyle, Barry 153
Drane, Robert 177, 182–4, 187

Eagleton, T 165
Eandly Challenge Cup 94
education 171
Edwards, Harry 22–3
egalitarianism 20
Elkin, AP 125, 127–8
Ella, May 21
Ella, Rodney 21
Erambie Allblacks
  1923 season 68–75
  'All Blacks' or 'Allblacks' 190n
  final years 94–8
  invitation matches 86–9
  origins 65–8
  re-emergence in 1970s 98
  representation of in newspapers 47, 65–80, 82–3, 86–9, 91–4, 99
  social significance of carnivals 32
Erambie Mission
  clever community members 146–8
  contact with Cowra residents 75–7
  disparity in conditions at 35
  fighting to resolve disputes 103–21
  focus on community 60
  haircutting at 39
  managed by Aborigines Protection Board 41–3
  manager attempts to expel Harry Murray 132, 134
  managers' perception of fights 103, 105–9, 119–20

oral history tradition 6, 39–40, 172–3
racism at 56–7
The Storyteller returns to 3
white manager appointed 76–7
Erenberg, L 157
Ethel (storyteller) 52, 58

Fanon, Frantz 75–6, 93–4, 98, 145, 164, 180, 186
Ferguson, Bill 134, 159
Fforde, C 14
fights, to resolve disputes 103–21, 172
  see also boxing
Flett, Jim 144
Flood, J 104
Folster, W 104
food rationing 57, 59
football 20, 28, 31–3, 96–7, 129, 141, 152–3, 169
Football: the first hundred years (Harvey) 169
Forbes 89, 94
Foster, J 106–8
Foucault, M 34
Frank (painter) 53
Freedom Rides 19
Freeman, Cathy 20

games 50–1
Gammage, B 40–1
Gardiner, Greg 24
Gardiner, Keith 141–2
Gems, G 128, 157
gidgewa 52
Gilbert, Kevin 19
Gleeson Cup 91, 94–5
Gleeson, Dan 95, 140
Globe Stadium, Cowra 141
Godwell, Darren 32–3, 47
gooligahs 50–1
Gordon (Erambie elder) 84–5
Gorman, Sean 24
Gorringe, S 14
Governor, Roy 71
Green, Danny 181–3, 187
Grenfell Record 90
grievance narratives 15, 25, 34
Griffith Area News 144
Grime, Billy 138
group discussions 47–8

INDEX

Group Nine Competition 95
gunyans 58

Haagen, C 50–1, 84
Hall, R 69
Hall, S 17, 23, 99, 125, 157–8, 186
Hallinan, Chris 30
Hamilton, D 92
Hardy, Stephen 170–1
Harper, D 45–6
Harrington, Kevin 179
Harris, Bret 21, 24
Harris, James 'Kid' 136
Harvey, Adrian 169
Hassen, Jack 19
Hawkins, Mick 140
Hay, R 169
Hazel (storyteller) 44, 48
Heads, Ian 66
Herald Sun 181
Hewstone, M 75
Hill, Jimmy 136
Hill, 'Snowy' 138
Hinton, P 75, 92
Hoberman, J 23
Holt, R 70
Horner, J 159
horse racing 30
household inspections 57–8, 133
Howitt, A 104
Hurst, Ted 136
hybridity 168–70
Hyslop, Jim 72–3

identity 14–15, 20–1, 23–6, 28, 30–3, 155–8, 163–4
illusory correlation, concept of 92
Ingamells, R 3
Ingram, Lachlan 'Diamond' 66, 80, 82, 150
Ingram, Nuggo 147
Ingram, S 49, 82
The Intervention 20
interviews 47

Jacobs, Ike 138
Jean (storyteller) 44
Jhally, S 157, 159
Jim (storyteller) 48–9, 80, 83
Jobson, Minister 132

Jopson, Debra 31–2
Jordan, George 143–4
Josie (storyteller) 35, 50, 54, 58–60, 114–16, 120, 133–4
Joyce (storyteller) 44
Judd, Barry 30
June (storyteller) 44–5, 48, 52, 55–6, 59–60
Jussim, I 68

Kane, J 20
Keating, P (author) 112
Keating, Paul 20
Kelton, Jim 104–5
Kennedy, Sam 79
Kenya 169–70
Kevin Cup 68
ki:ka:wi:lan 126
'king plates' 126, 128
Kinnear, Bobby 27, 163
Knockout (rugby) 30–1
Kogoy, Peter 181
Koorawatha rugby team 71, 78–9
Kosuth, B 119

La Perouse, Sydney 21
Labor League 43
Lachlan (boxer) 117–18, 133
Lachlan Leader 95–7, 106–7, 151–2
Lachlan River 3, 40–1, 51–2, 77
Land Rights Acts 19
Langton, Marcia 14–15, 35
language 75–6, 92–4, 125
  see also Wiradjuri language
Lansdown, H 80
Leab, D 93
Lee, Horace 141
Lee, Y 68
legends 51–3, 56, 61
Lewis, Johnny 181
Lithgow Mercury 140
Louis, Joe 156, 190n
Love, Stan 139
Lynch, Jack 139

MacDonald, Dick 141
Macdonald, G 39, 43, 109–12, 165–8, 170
Macquarie, Lachlan 103–4
Maher Cup 68, 95–8
Mandurama Reds 77–80, 86–7

203

Margaret (storyteller) 44–5, 48, 52
Marqusee, M 93
marriage 52
Marriott, J 40, 105
Marsh, Larry 130
Martin, G 104
Masters, R 80
Matilda (storyteller) 58
Mavis (storyteller) 44–5, 47, 51, 53–4, 56–60, 66, 75, 108, 113, 145–6, 155, 172–4
Maynard, John 30
Mazawi, A 14
McAdam, Adrian 29
McAdam, Charlie 29
McAdam family 28–9
McAdam, Gilbert 29
McAdam, Greg 29
McCarthy, Darby 24–5, 180
McCauley, C 68
McCoy, Brian 28, 31
McGregor, R 128
McGuinness, Billy 154
McGuinness, Denise 155
McGuinness, Gertie 146
McGuinness, Ken 154
McGuinness, Kevin 154
McGuinness, Richard 'Dicky' 96–7, 154
McGuinness, Teddy 154
McHugh, Pat 141
McKenna, M 23
McKnight, D 112
McLaren, Enid 57
Memmi, A 186
Merritt, Moodie 53
Millie (storyteller) 44–5, 50, 174
Miranda, Dick 141, 143
Mirrihula 49, 51
missions 42
   see also Erambie Mission; Warangesda Mission
Morgan, Bob 31–2
'movement culture' 169–70
Moy, Charlie 'Kid' 138
Mulvaney, DJ 18–19
Mulyan Reserve 41–2, 129
Mundine, Anthony 4, 177, 181–4, 187
Murray, Alan 90, 148
Murray, Claude 139, 146, 148
Murray family, generally 125–6, 155–60

Murray, Foley 146
Murray, Frank 148
Murray, Harry James 'Jim' 72, 79, 96, 128, 150–4, 159
Murray, Harry 'Major' 54, 59, 66–7, 71–2, 74–5, 78, 91–2, 95–7, 133, 146–8, 159
Murray, Harry senior 48, 65–6, 83–5, 95, 107, 128–34, 151, 190n
Murray, Herbert 'Doolan' 66–7, 69, 74–5, 97, 133–50, 155–7, 159, 182
Murray, Jane 83–4, 95, 132–3
Murray, Ollie 133
Murray, Sam 65, 85, 129, 190n
Murray, Viney 96, 149
Murrumbidgee River 40–1
Musgrave, Sarah 105
music 54–5, 60, 87–8, 90

Nakata, Martin 17–18, 29
Narrandera 43
Narrandera Gift 152
Narrundjera clan 40
National Advocate 148
National Apology 20
Native Americans 129, 157
native title 20
Nelson, Alison 26
Newham, Joe 137
newspaper articles
   as memory-aides 47
   representation of Aborigines in 65–80, 82–3, 86–99, 106–7, 125, 130–3, 135, 153–4, 158–9, 181
   see also names of specific newspapers
Newton, Reuben 81
Ngunnawal clan 41–2, 52
Ngunnawal language 58
Norma (storyteller) 44, 49–50, 53, 174
Norman, Heidi 30–2
Nowhere people (Reynolds) 190n

Oates, Joyce Carol 183–4
Obstacle race... (Tatz) 22
Olympic Games (2000) 20
Onus, Eric 91
oral history 49
   see also storytelling
Outcasts (group) 55
Oxley Cup 68

INDEX

Pascoe, Sid 140
Pearl (storyteller) 58
Pearson, Noel 13-15, 171-3
Perry, Dave 66
Perry, John 27, 163
Phillips, Nathan 178
photographs, as a resource 45-7
Pickering, M 93-4
Pioneers 66-7, 69-74, 76-7, 82-3, 87, 89, 91, 95
Pollard, Jack 19
Pollard, Vince 139
Protectors of Aborigines 41
pugilism *see* boxing

Quandialla 87

race, as a 'floating signifier' 99, 157, 186
racial classification 158-9
Racial Discrimination Act 20
racism
   confronting 14
   demonstrating unfairness of 20
   at Erambie Mission 56-7
   in newspaper reporting 69, 73-5, 77, 89-91
   portrayal of Muhammad Ali 183-4
   in sport 22-6, 33, 67-8, 70, 73, 89, 153, 177-8, 180
   stories about 56-7, 179-80
   and victimhood 13
   white explanations of black prowess 155-60
Railway (football team) 97
Read, H 78
Read, P 42-3, 50, 76, 80, 84, 133, 155
Redfern speech (Keating) 20
Reds *see* Mandurama Reds
Reed, A 103
The Referee 66
referendum (1967) 18
Reidy, George 136
reserves, life on 42-4
   see also Erambie Mission; Warangesda Mission
Reynolds, Henry 190n
Richards, Ron 19
Rigney, Daryle 30
Rimas-Kabaila, P 75

ritualised fighting 103-4, 109, 112, 119
Rose, Lionel 19
Ross, J 14
'roundies' 50
Royal Commission into Aboriginal Deaths in Custody (1991) 20
Ruck, R 80
rugby 30-1, 65-6, 68, 95, 153
   see also Cowra Pioneers; Erambie Allblacks; Mandurama Reds
running 27, 129-31, 150-1, 169-70
Russell, I 128
Russell, Lynette 26, 31
Ryan, Jimmy 140

Sailes, G 70
Sammons, JT 25
Sang, J 169-70
schools 171
The Science of Man (journal) 84
Sharman, Jimmy 105, 143-4
Shaw, 'Buck' 136
Shepparton Gift 153
Shepparton News 153
Sherif, C 76
Sherif, M 76
Shields, C 14
Shields, D 177
Shirley (storyteller) 81-2
Simpson, Frank 53-4
Simpson, JR 152
Simpson, Vic 150
skipping games 50-1, 85
Slicaa, H 47-8
Smith, Bob 32
Smith, Fred 139
Smith, S 65, 82
social Darwinism 129
social inclusion, and sport 80-6
songs 53-4, 60
Southern Cross (newspaper) 87-8
Spillius, A 80
sport *see* Aborigines in sport; *names of specific sports*
sprinting 27, 129-31
St Kilda Football Club 97
St Raphael's Handicap 135
Stammers, L 73
Standpoint Theory 29

INDEX

Stanley, Jim 139
Stanner, WEH 19
Stawell Gift 130–1
Stawell News 130
stereotypes, of Aborigines 14–15, 19, 68, 75–7, 89–94, 98–9, 179, 182, 184
Stolen Generations 56–7, 172
The Storyteller 3–5, 45, 47–9, 54, 66, 80–1, 94–5, 125, 156, 159
storytelling 4–5, 44–5, 49–52, 83, 166, 172–3
Sydney Morning Herald 31, 181
Sykes, R 65, 82
Sylvia (storyteller) 44, 47, 49, 57, 81, 84, 113, 133, 154

Tatz, C 13, 16, 21–4, 26, 70, 129
Tatz, P 13, 23–4, 129
Taylor, P 49
Temora Gift 151
tent boxing 143
Tent Embassy 19
Thomas, Faith 27
Thomas, Ted 141
Thompson, EP 25
Tom (Erambie resident) 75
Tom (tent boxer) 112
tradition 167–8, 186
Tregenza, Elizabeth 28–9
tribalism 80–1
Troy, J 126

United States 128–9

Vamplew, W 23–4
victimhood 13–15, 185–6
Victorian Football League 97

walemira 126–7
Walker, C 55
Wallace, Florence 147
Walmsley, K 119
Warangesda Mission 42
Washington, Booker T 15
Watt, Stuart 182
Wattamondra 91–2

Wegner, Ulli 181
Western District Sheffield Handicaps 131
Western Sun 89, 94
Whimpress, Bernard 27, 30, 169–70
Whitty, Ernest 'Buffalo' 66, 91, 146, 155
Whitty, Josie 147
Wilga (storyteller) 54–5
Williams, A (sprinter) 152
Williams, Alfred 'Knocker' 42, 54–5, 66
Williams, Arthur 150
Williams, Harry 54–5
Williams, Mervyn 79, 96
Williams, Mr (boxer) 137
Williams, Nino 150
Williams, Peter 150
Williams, Ray (footballer) 96
Williams, Raymond (author) 165–6
willy-wagtails 52
Wilson, Alex 149
Wiltshire, Clive 153
Winmar, Nicky 24
Wiradjuri language 52, 58
Wiradjuri people
  the *bidja* 128–34, 170, 172
  conflict with reserve managers 76–7
  contact with people of Cowra 75
  cultural continuity 165–71, 187
  exceptional Wiradjuri men 126–7, 159
  fighting to resolve disputes 103–21, 172
  history of 39–44
  identity formation 163–4
  oral tradition 49–50
  sporting culture 84, 99
  storytelling about legends 51–3, 56, 61
  territoriality of 80–1
  traditional games 50–1, 84–5
  traditional movement patterns 42
  see also Erambie Mission
wiri:nan 126
Woodstock rugby team 69
The wretched of the earth (Fanon) 76

Yass 42
Young Daily Witness 90–1, 94

'Come on Martin [Jim's nickname], we'll give you two or three yards, pace make for us'. 'No, no!' [indicating that he did not want a head start]. They give me three yards. Boom! They said, 'we can't give this fella three yards'. I had no boots on and they had the shorts and the running spikes. They had the works.

Some time later, while he still going to school, Jim's grandfather (Harry Murray senior) introduced Jim to professional sprinting during a community sports carnival in Cowra:

At the St Patrick's Day races...So, poor old Grandfather [Harry Murray] was there and he said, 'I entered Martin [Jim] in the foot-running'. He said, 'you want to go and see them'...So away I go down to the track and these fellows came out in their knicks [knickerbockers, racing tights], running shoes, shiny skin like a brand new penny. Lochie, Victor, Nino, so anyway the wusname [handicapper] give me the handicap. He said, 'this fellow's running off six yards'. [Of] course, they started bucking about that saying, 'we can't give this fella six yards'. They said, 'we can't give him one yard'. He said, 'it doesn't make any difference what you can't do, that's his mark. He's still a schoolboy'. So they said, 'we'll save five bob with ya'. I said, 'no youse won't'. I said, 'you beat me and you keep all the money'. It was worth ten pound. Ten pound made you a millionaire in those days...They couldn't beat me that day with a shanghai and a tree.

Newspaper articles tracked Jim Murray's rise as a sprinter and rugby league player. These articles are an example of the way the representation of Erambie athletes could change according to circumstances. Jim had success early in his sprinting career and was praised in the *Lachlan Leader* (hereafter *Leader*) as a 'Cowra boy'. He won 21 pounds by finishing second in the final of the 75 yards as well as the 120-yard Temora Gift final. It was reported in the *Leader* that 'experienced critics were enthusiastic over his performance and predicted that a lot would be seen of him on N.S.W. foot-running tracks in the next few years' (1 January 1940).

In March Jim gave an exhibition run at the West Cowra Recreation Ground where he ran evens time — 10 seconds for 100 yards, which is a measure of ability over sprint distances. The *Leader* article termed him 'Cowra's champion sprinter':

The run was an exhibition one…A. Williams paced Murray, receiving about ten yards start. Murray passed him when little more than half the distance had been covered. Three watches were on the run, each registering ten seconds. This is the same time recorded by Murray at Temora sports meeting recently. It will be his last public run before starting in the Narrandera Gift meeting Easter Monday. (18 March 1940)

A front-page *Leader* article from March 1940 reported Jim Murray's running ability to the Cowra public (28 March). The article is noteworthy for two reasons. First, it reinforces the athletic ability of another member of the Murray family. Second, Murray is at this stage termed 'Cowra's champion sprinter', which indicates a link to the town at a time when Aborigines were not generally welcome in town.

Jim's effort in finishing second in the 75 yards race at Narrandera was reported with the claim that 'the Cowra runner's win in the semi-final was popular'. The *Leader* reported that 'another of Doolan Murray's protégés', JR Simpson, also competed in this event (28 March 1940). Jim was still 'Cowra's champion' at this stage and in this article was termed 'Cowra's champion rugby league winger'. In the same edition another headline claimed he would possibly leave the football team to play Australian rules football in Melbourne:

It is not yet known for certain whether Jim will accept the offer. It is known that he doubts his ability in the Australian code. His father 'Doolan' is of the opinion that Jimmy might turn the offer down. (28 March 1940)

By May, Jim had decided he would not play football for Cowra. Instead he returned to Victoria to live. Jim's account of this time indicated he was not happy with his treatment in the town.

There was a subtle change in references to Jim when it became clear that he would not return to play for Cowra. The *Leader* article covering the story that he would not return to the team called Jim 'Cowra's colored [sic] winger' (13 May 1940). Later in the article, when discussing a conversation between the reporter and Doolan Murray, Jim was reported to have been 'dissatisfied with the treatment accorded him in Cowra'. Jim was then called 'the dusky winger'.

Jim's account of his departure highlights that he was dissatisfied with his treatment when playing rugby league in Cowra:

> They [Cowra Football Club] come up to the mission and wanted me to play. Grandfather said 'no'. He said, 'you're not taking him'...I said, 'I'm off', and this was when Cowra had a good side...I went down to Victoria and started playing that 'aerial ping-pong'...I stopped there and played for City United in Shepparton and I was getting about ten pound to play football. So that's what happened. I stayed there and played football there...Anyway, later, they wanted me to play and I said, 'I'll play one more season with Cowra, on one condition'...Every Saturday when we used to play at home and they had a side gate. This was for the mission. I said, 'no dice, my people go in the main gate, not in that side gate. You can lock it, you can do what you like, fence it in'. I said, 'if one goes in there that will finish me. Those days are gone, they're not going to be walking in side gates'.

Jim remained in Shepparton where he played Australian rules and trained teams there and in Wangaratta until his health failed. On 12 March 1999, the *Guardian* sports editor, Barry Doyle, praised Jim for his accomplishments when representing the town, in a series of articles that profiled his career. He wrote that Jim Murray was a 'local league legend' and '[a] true gentleman'.

In Victoria, Jim was also known for his athletic ability and his race. He was known for his all-round sporting ability and he told me that his nickname was the 'Black Prince'. Richard Broome gave the following description of Jim's career in Victoria in his 2005 history, *Aboriginal Victorians: A history from 1880*:

> Harry James (Jimmy) Murray was a fine professional runner in the 1940s. His trainer, Clive Wiltshire, believed he was unfairly handicapped in the Shepparton Gift in 1945 at a crucial time in his career, preventing him from becoming 'one of Australia's really great runners'. Lynchy Cooper agreed, remarking that in his prime, Murray 'could have downed the best Australian runners'. He was still running well in 1950, achieving five firsts and a second in one week. The *Shepparton News* praised his abilities in several sports and referred to him as a 'fine ambassador to his race' and 'an acquisition to any

community'. Sport thus had the power to transform, for this praise was given to Murray at the same time as the Aboriginal campers were being called a 'menace' to the Shepparton community. (Broome 2005: 270)

The way Jim was described in the Shepparton newspaper paralleled the way he and his family were written about in Cowra's newspapers. In both cases the Murray athletes were represented in contrast to the 'menace' of their race. Broome attributes this to sport when he says 'Aboriginal people gained power and prestige from sport to counter the hurts of being Aboriginal in a town that disparaged them' (2005: 270). Broome's reference to Jim Murray indicates two things. First, Jim Murray demonstrated his sporting ability in a number of sports. Second, he earned an identity that went against the normal way Aborigines were portrayed. Unlike Broome, I think this reputation went beyond his athletic abilities. Both Cowra and Shepparton had a number of outstanding Koori athletes. However, in both cases the Murray family stood out. At the time, in the 1950s, Jim was an 'ambassador to his race' whereas in Cowra his family were still being denied their Aboriginality when they did not fit stereotypes of Aborigines. One possible explanation for this could be that Jim did not come from the area and that his positive identity was possible without conceding the same characteristics to the local Aborigines, who could remain a 'menace'.

A number of branches of the Murray family remained prominent in the local Cowra sporting community. Some of Doolan's sisters' children and grandchildren were also elite athletes. For example, Richard 'Dicky' McGuinness is a legendary local football player. Sylvia recalled Dicky's ability in a way that is indicative of the stories told about the Murray family:

> The one I remember the most was Dicky. Gee he could play football. I remember one game over here at the West Cowra ground he ran from one end to the other and scored and he dodged them all and they couldn't even touch him. He was fast and he dodged them all, like a rabbit, he was.

Dicky's younger brother Teddy reached the top of Australian boxing as his uncle Doolan had done three decades before, by becoming a contender for an Australian title. Dicky's son Billy is remembered as an exceptionally talented rugby league player. Dicky's grandsons Ken and Kevin McGuinness reached the highest level of Australian and English rugby league. Doolan's grand nieces Denise McGuinness and Isobel Coe were national and state representative basketball players. Each successive generation has built on the reputation of the Murray family as athletes.

Less than half-caste

The achievements of the Murray family contradicted the prevailing ideas about Aborigines. Their highly visible achievements on the sporting field required explanation. Explanations of black achievements often revolve around racial identity. The questions about the Murray's Aboriginality are central to the way their story is told both within and outside of the Erambie community.

Reports by an Aborigines Protection Board manager that there was a strong strain of Negro blood in the Murray family, and that generally classify the community as lesser-caste Aborigines, are read by Margaret and June as possibly being attempts to undermine their family's authority within the community.[4] The managers tempered their reports of positive aspects of community life with denials of Aboriginality. Erambie residents often respond angrily to these denials of the Murray's Aboriginality or any suggestion that they were anything other than full-blooded Wiradjuri. It is apparent that the identity of this family remains a relevant issue to some people.

Senior Erambie women and men also grow angry at Board reports that attribute positive aspects of the community to white people. Credit for the football team, the fine community band and the thriving social life have been attributed to the manager, the matron, to the mission being close to the town, and even to an alleged Negro heritage of community leaders. Crediting the manager for the football team and band ignores the fact that both were part of the community before the managers were appointed in 1924. The message is clear: Aborigines were not capable of managing their own communities so their achievements needed explanation. In contrast, within the Erambie community men like Doolan are remembered as respected elders, leaders and examples of the 'smartness' of Wiradjuri people. Mavis said of her elders: 'Uncle Doolan, Gertie, Nan, Uncle Cutter, Buffalo Whitty and them, they ran things and it was a good place to live'. Agnes agreed that '[t]he older people ran the mission' in spite of the managers (in Read 1984a: 67).

The floating signifier

There are noticeable contrasts in the meanings that are attributed to the achievements of Erambie people. There are a number of ways the achievements and events can be viewed. Examples from other contexts can contribute to understanding the significance of black people's victories and achievements in sport.

African-American author Maya Angelou wrote of Joe Louis' success: 'Champion of the world. A black boy. Some black mother's son. He was the strongest man in the world' (Angelou 1984: 132). In contrast to the way some black people saw Louis, Myler found 'Joe's skin color dominated almost every description of him...Dark Destroyer, the Panther with the pin-cushion lips, the Brown Bomber' (Myler 2005: 44). For the two groups, white and black, Louis represented an alternate view of race. For some he was depicted in a way that emphasised fear and the unknown, while Erenberg suggested that for others he was '[a] successful black superhero' who 'offered a new myth of masculine strength to wipe out memories of slavery' (2006: 4).

In the racial climate of early twentieth century Cowra, Doolan Murray's boxing victories undoubtedly helped to validate the identity of many Aborigines. It was explained to me that Doolan was a hero to his people because he represented Wiradjuri Kooris during his fights. The esteem in which the Storyteller held Doolan Murray was evident when he said with heavy irony:

> Couldn't fight much. Aww mate, he could throw 'em. They could all fight in them days, the men from the mission. Daddy and them used to go and watch him [Doolan] fight. They'd travel with him, to you know, watch him. They all followed him back then.

For Wiradjuri people, the Murrays are an example of the worth of Wiradjuri culture. In contrast, newspaper writers often considered Doolan Murray's athletic body in terms of racial thought. Doolan's physical appearance was to be marvelled at and he was described, as a race horse might be, as flesh to be admired for its physical wonder. The following example from the *Cootamundra Liberal* illustrates:

> Even those who take no interest in fisticuffs will have noticed the fine physical lines of the young aboriginal, 'Doolan' Murray. His fine supple form, the graceful curves of his limbs, the perfectly moulded

proportions of his young manhood. With these go his clean shiny skin, beautiful black hair, perfect ivory teeth. But even of more interest to note, as one could not fail to do, the kindly nature of the lad — his exceedingly pleasant smile, the gentleness of the lad — almost it might be written the gentlemanliness, for 'Doolan', though he punches so well, does not belong to the bumptious, flash and aggressive order. The writer questioned whether he could be 'full-blood'. The reply was that the Cowra boy was believed to be a true son of Australia. (10 August 1921)

Similar observations have been made in other context. Boxing victories of Native Americans have been viewed within the context of the 'culture of defeat' that Erenberg describes (2006: 64–5). Using oral history, Bloom identified boxing as a forum for expressing a strong sense of pride among Native Americans who were keen to show their abilities (2000). Gems examined the negotiation and transformation of racial identity in the context of white characterisation of Native Americans and black Americans. He suggested that sport played a central role in the process of negotiation of identity as it was one of the few areas of social interaction between whites and natives (1999).

The Murrays' identity and achievements needed to be explained or excused in terms of racial thought. For the Board, the Murrays needed to be represented in relation to the negative stereotypes about Aborigines that underpinned their continued control. To the Board, the Murrays were of Negro blood rather than Aboriginal. This connects with Hall's argument that the concept of race is best aligned with shared historical experiences and that race itself is a 'floating signifier' which is context dependent (in Jhally 1996). In the United States, Negro achievements in sport were represented in negative ways. However, in the Australian context, some of the achievements of the Erambie community were explained by claiming that the Negro blood predominated. The meaning attached to the signifiers of race is altered according to context.

A central part of Hall's argument is that race should be viewed not as a biological concept but as a discursive production of language (in Jhally 1996). Hall's suggestion that race is more like a language than a biological makeup is interesting to consider in relation to the way the Murrays were and are known.

There are contrasting constructions of identity for the Murray family where their abilities are explained in various ways, from not being Aborigines to confirming their Wiradjuri identity. This, as Hall suggests, is rooted as much in historical, shared experiences for members of the Erambie community as it is in biology or genetic markers of race. That is, the Murrays' identity is constructed within the Erambie community as an example of what is good about Wiradjuri culture and society. The language used to represent Wiradjuri athletes is an example of identity construction that is context dependant.

This varied identity construction is linked not just to experiences with white people but as a part of 'traditional' Wiradjuri culture before contact. The storytellers represent the exceptional as heroes in much the same way as their ancestors had done. The way the Murray family identity is constructed is therefore, for some people, an example of continuation or persistence of an undated Wiradjuri culture. On the other hand, they are represented by outsiders in a way that disconnects them from their culture.

Hall also borrows from anthropologist Mary Douglas' concept of 'matter out of place' to explain his ideas about changes in representation of race. Hall interprets Douglas' idea of matter out of place in the following way:

> Every culture has an order of classification built into it and this seems to stabilise a culture. You know exactly where you are, you know who are the inferiors and who the superiors are. How each has a rank. What disturbs you is what she [Douglas] calls matter out of place. When things don't symbolically belong in certain places. This leads to a need to restore the fixed boundaries between what belongs and what does not, inside–outside, cultured–uncultured, barbarous and cultivated, and so on (in Jhally 1996).

The Murray family's identity is appropriated to restore boundaries both within the community and for outsiders. For the Erambie community they are represented in a way that restores the classification of Wiradjuri identity in a positive light. In contrast, when the Murrays disturb the boundaries between Wiradjuri community and the white community their identity is changed, by white commentators, to restore these boundaries and maintain the hierarchy that places Wiradjuri below whites. The consistent representations of their character, as identified in their sporting achievements in newspaper accounts, did not fit the idea of racial hierarchy promoted by the Aborigines Welfare Board and its predecessor. The managers of the Board attempted firstly to counter the Murrays' reputation by suggesting they did not deserve the reputation they had and were of bad character, as other Aborigines were. When that did not work they resorted to denying their Aboriginality by claiming there was a strong strain of Negro blood which overshadowed the Wiradjuri. The Murray family was being reclassified and separated from the other mission residents in a way that restored the order and refixed the boundaries.

As Hall suggests, the power of racial classification 'is a function of a common sense code in society' and that people fit so neatly into these categories that common sense arguments are not even needed to maintain them (in Jhally 1996). Aborigines, consistent with racial thinking, were of sound body, good dancers, very expressive but lacking intelligence and prone to the barbarous behaviour of the noble savage (Hall, in Jhally 1996). The identity of a group can be altered to suit an argument or ideology to maintain the status quo or effect changes.

Jim and his sisters spoke about their knowledge of a Wiradjuri clever man named Budjarn who they knew to have powers that included being able to *bahloo* (kill) people using strands of their hair. This type of clever man had the knowledge of mystical powers that Elkin had claimed were no longer around. The Storyteller and Bill Ferguson described another type of Wiradjuri clever man when they recalled the abilities of the Murray family. Ferguson recalled the identity of the Murray family in his 1994 biography, 'Erambie was famous for its athletes, especially the Murray family' (in Horner 1994: 73). The Storyteller repeatedly described the Murray men in the following way:

> Oh they were smart men, never swore. I remember, Uncle Major, Uncle Doolan, Jimmy Murray. I remember, very clever men. They could do anything, run, fight, sing. They were smart [educated] too. You name it, they could do it. Oh mate, they was smart men. Very smart men.

The Storyteller encouraged me to record the achievements of some of our heroes. In doing this, some obvious themes emerged in the way these men were represented. This was the case within the Erambie community as well as in the documentary sources that were produced by outsiders. Attempts were made in the outsider representations to dissociate the Murray family from Wiradjuri people when they did not conform to the way Aborigines were represented. Again, a contrast was apparent with the way they were represented within the community. For Erambie people, the Murray family represents an example of all that is good about our culture. So, while outsiders attempted to claim that this family excelled in so many areas because they were of Negro heritage, to the people of Erambie they excelled precisely because they were Wiradjuri. They were continuing a Wiradjuri tradition of clever men who excelled in many areas. The way the Murray men were represented further indicates the frictions that are present in the way we are known within and outside of our community. These representations also further indicate the imbalance that exists in the way knowledge about us is constructed, in that our representations of ourselves remain largely unknown to outsiders.

Chapter 6

Representation: Words and people

> But so far we have only heard the white voice on paternalism and the place of Aboriginal people in a bygone era. It was essential to hear about Kinnear from the other side of the racial divide...Aboriginal informants did not harp on the theme of pathos so central to white depictions of their people. Kinnear had not remained in black memory as a pathetic old man...Bobbie Kinnear had definitely not been 'Poor Old Bobbie'. Rather, he was a sort of repository of knowledge and a valued elder statesman. (Perry 2002: 190)

The dominant discourse on Aborigines in sport is about deficit, and rarely does that discourse reflect my own positive experiences with sport on Erambie Mission. The essence of Indigenous experiences in sport is almost never written about — community togetherness fostered by games and sport, or the significant role played by elders in encouraging participation in and enjoyment of games and sports. Nor do we read about community elders' aspirations to teach young people the value of 'the old people's ways' that are transmitted though sport and physical activities. The problem is not that racism or social breakdown are uncovered in research about minorities; rather, what is problematic in that they are too often the only stories told.

The stories I am familiar with indicate that racism alone cannot account for the sporting experiences of Wiradjuri people. Similarly, Cashill's singular attribution of the success of minority athletes to family influences, minimising or denying the role of racism, is equally problematic (2006). Borrowing from a number of ideas helped to explain what I was observing and hearing. While I concede that the choices I have made in relation to theoretical frameworks may have been influenced by my preconceived ideas, the themes regarding cultural continuity do exist, and as such the choices I made to explain them were grounded in the words of the senior men and women who told me their stories. In this book, my choices as a researcher and a community member have contributed to what has emerged and in that sense the people telling the stories and I are speaking together.

While I am concerned with uncovering the truth of past events, my primary focus is on the representation of events and people. It is, after all, representations of the past that produce histories as they are read and told. I have drawn on writers who have explicitly considered the production of knowledge about colonised and indigenous peoples as their ideas could be of use in this study. My understanding of the data and my own informal theories suggested that ideas about power over knowledge and reactions from within the colonised communities could be useful in framing my analysis. However, I did have questions about how the data should be interpreted. Was there, for instance, only one way indigenous peoples could interpret data about the way we were known?

Agreeing with the idea that it appears to be important for whites to manage the identity of blacks, I sought to uncover how Wiradjuri people respond to these representations in terms of their own identity formation. I wanted to know how and why Wiradjuri people self-identified in certain ways. Having some understanding of how the 'other' may have contributed to this process was important. Establishing the level of white intrusion into the lives of the Wiradjuri was also important because I was interested in connections with a time before colonisation. I wanted to gauge the impact of whites on the Wiradjuri culture as well as how the representations of those outsiders may have influenced how our people viewed themselves.

Fanon puts forward the argument that 'the black man has two dimensions; one with his fellows, the other with the white man' (1952/1970: 13). This idea about identity formation among people who are forced to contend with outside representations from a coloniser offers a way to examine how individual and group identities were formed. The idea that a black person has a dimension among 'his fellows' provided a way of examining the interaction of concepts such as representation and continuity. Comparisons exist between the way Wiradjuri people saw themselves in relation to white people's ideas about them as well as in relation to the past.

Continuity

Continuity, as it relates to studies of the cultures of indigenous people, emerged from anthropological research. It is usually used in reference to changes and consistencies in indigenous cultures. For colonised indigenous people, the issue of cultural continuity relates directly to cultural authenticity and identity. However, cultural continuity is also a question of interpretation and representation. The term culture itself has many uses. Macdonald has researched Wiradjuri culture for more than two decades and, for her, the concepts of culture and continuity should be understood in historical terms. Her definition of culture includes 'those social, intellectual and materially-orientated practices through which people express what it means to them to be in the world' (2001: 182). She goes on to argue that culture is the product of people's interactions with each other and their environments. Environment or location is also an important element of Eagleton's definition of culture. He writes that culture is a sliding concept due to the varied meanings that are attached to it and that anthropologists call culture the way of life of a group of people living together in one place (Eagleton 2000). The idea of culture as the ordinary of everyday life is summed up by Raymond Williams:

> Culture is ordinary: that is the first fact. Every human society has its own shape, its own purposes, its own meanings, every human society expresses these, in institutions, and in arts and learning. The making of a society is the finding of common meanings and directions…We use the word culture in these two senses: to mean a whole way of life — the common meanings; to mean the arts and learning…The questions I ask about culture are questions about general and common purposes, yet also questions about deep personal meanings. Culture is ordinary, in every society and in every mind. (1993: 6)

These definitions of culture share an emphasis on meanings or that people themselves determine how they express themselves. This book is derived from my interest in the way community elders saw our shared culture. It is from them that I got my initial ideas about what it meant to be Wiradjuri. The contrasting ways that our culture is seen make an emphasis on individual and group understanding important, as these differences are central in the

Wiradjuri identities that this book examines. Sport and acts of physical skill are central or normal to everyday life within the community. What is of interest, then, are the ways the ordinary aspects of our lives are known.

The concept of continuity, when used in relation to Australia's Indigenous cultures, has emerged from ideas about the breakdown and subsequent loss of culture. In fact, from what I read, the term continuity came into use as an alternative to discontinuity. I agree with Macdonald when she writes that almost all anthropological work on south-eastern Australian Aborigines up until the 1970s reinforced the notion of discontinuity, or that classical Aboriginal culture was a thing of the past (2001: 182). She goes on to argue that this situation came from the misguided emphasis that researchers and observers placed on rituals and spirituality and that led to social practices being ignored. The survival of Indigenous cultures, such as that of the Wiradjuri, has been judged on only part of the social and cultural life, while the 'ordinary' of Williams' definition has been ignored. Therefore, continuity entered the discourse on Indigenous cultures in this country as a result of the acceptance of breakdown and loss.

Wiradjuri history can be divided according to contact with Europeans. This includes the pre-invasion and settlements periods through to the mission era and beyond, to an era of less restriction. I am dealing primarily with the pre-invasion and mission eras. The everyday aspects of Wiradjuri culture that, Macdonald argues, demonstrate continuity from the pre-colonisation period were identified primarily during her 1980s research. Examining a storytelling tradition that spans all of the eras mentioned meant looking at the period that covered the transition from pre-invasion to mission culture. In this sense the temporal connection between the 'traditional' culture and the practices on Erambie in this book is less fractured than in Macdonald's study, which was over a century removed from the 'traditional'. This point is important as it makes judging logical connections between the two eras less problematic than it would be when a greater time period is covered. The extent that continuity exists over time is addressed in the stories told in this book.

The use of the concept of continuity rests on accepting that meaning is as important as, or even more important than, observable cultural actions. If we accept the importance of meaning, then continuity can be demonstrated if meanings can be shown to be continued. In order to consider continuity of indigenous cultures that have previously been considered to have lost contact with the past, Macdonald suggests two major shifts in approach. The first involves thinking of indigenous cultures as dynamic and continually evolving rather than the static, unchanging model previously considered authentic. Authenticity is a key term: a contemporary culture may be considered authentic despite an apparently observable disconnection from an idealised past. What Macdonald is suggesting is that a continuity of culture may be present in the meanings attached to evolving cultural practices. Her stance on the way indigenous cultures should be approached can be seen in the following quote:

> A model of culture that assumes a people's life ways are characterised only by immediately observable activities is one that cannot take into account the meanings, values and the inter-relationships between activities. (Macdonald 2001: 185)

In addition to redefining cultures as dynamic, Macdonald also re-interprets the term tradition in her use of continuity. For her, there is a need to look beyond 'surface' or 'manifest' culture to the meanings to redefine traditionality which has thus far been associated with the material artefacts of indigenous cultures. The concept of tradition, then, has to be reconciled for continuity to work because the understanding of what is traditional to indigenous cultures has narrowly focused on certain artefacts and practices. 'Tradition' is a burden south-eastern Aborigines have to bear because it carries with it a subtext of authenticity and Aborigines are asked to prove authenticity by proving traditionality. Whereas Macdonald is critical of this process, I do not consider proving our authenticity problematic. What is a problem, however, is when we are not allowed to define what constitutes a Wiradjuri person or culture.

Macdonald's use of tradition as including 'those practices and beliefs of a people which are regarded as having been informed by practices or beliefs of the past' allows for the inclusion of early-contact Wiradjuri culture as well as of more recent acquisitions (2001: 188). This is done by using a strategic definition of tradition that takes a dynamic rather than a static approach, similar to the way she defines culture. As long as traditions originally came from Wiradjuri culture, acquisitions do not diminish the concept of continuity. My approach had been to compare the observable aspects of 'traditional culture' with those of the mission era as well as examining the meanings or ideas that mission-era Wiradjuri hold about our way of being. Continuity and the redefined approaches it offers have been used to make sense of what I observed and of the oral testimony that examines the meanings attached to the observably distinct nature of our culture. Macdonald's approach to continuity is attractive for this reason. In her work I could identify not only the recognisable events and phenomena but the interpretations of why they occurred.

Discontinuity as the antithesis of continuity leads to some other commonly used frameworks in examining indigenous cultures. To be useful in this context, continuity must also confront the idea of indigenous cultures being hybrid. If discontinuity is the direct opposite of continuity then hybridity is the concept that explains the observable differences between white culture and the remnant of the discontinued culture under examination. On this point, Macdonald writes:

> Aspects of Aboriginal cultural traditions cannot be understood as inversions or transformations of introduced forms, but as transformations and practices and meanings with a history distinct from, albeit significantly shaped by, the presence and pressures of European colonisers. (2001: 177)

A hybrid culture implies some substantial loss of tradition while explaining differences as mainly being related to socio-economic factors. Macdonald makes this connection when she argues that studies of culture from the 1960s characterised Aborigines as being 'just like groups of poor whites' (2001: 177). This explains the differences of indigenous communities in relation to white society and disconnects us from the past so, while I accept that some similarities exist between all groups of outsiders, I do not consider Wiradjuri culture to be 'just like [that of] poor whites'. Using the concept of hybridity to frame explanations of indigenous cultures implies that cultures from south-eastern Australia can be viewed only in this way.

It should be noted that constructions of indigenous histories and identities often have political uses (Adair 2006). It appears that hybridity entered the literature on Aborigines as a result of the belief in discontinuity. When the mission culture of many Indigenous groups remained observably different, the idea gradually emerged of a hybridisation of the traditional culture that was guided by socio-economic factors. In this model, sport is not only considered to provide evidence for, but is also an agent of, social control of indigenous groups by imperial colonisers. That is, sport is an agent in the destruction of indigenous cultures.

Identifying examples of continuity is not new to sports history. Hay outlines how he and others examined and identified continuity in British football. In his review of Adrian Harvey's 2005 *Football the first hundred years: The untold story*, Hay argues that questions of 'disruption or continuity' and 'invention and transmission' are tackled head on (2006: 77–8). He also states that 'persistences' (continuity of practices and meanings) were identified in football as it transitioned from the 'popular' form of the game to the codified version that the public-school educated Britons exported around the world (79). Ultimately, Hay found the idea of football as a form of 'cultural continuity' convincing.

In another example of continuity being used as a framework to explain sport, Bale and Sang set up some important definitions of terms that must be reconciled in any examination of continuity of indigenous cultures. In this examination of the success of Kenyan distance runners, continuity is considered in relation to a specific definition of 'ancient' and modern sports. Bale and Sang write that Kenya's 'movement culture' can be divided into the traditions of 'tribal folk activities' and 'globalised modern sport' (1996: 47–72). Wiradjuri sport consists of both the folk activities Bale and Sang identified in Kenyan culture and competitive sports such as football, which was played between clan and tribal groups. Although the concept of continuity has been used in sports history, it has not yet been seriously considered in the context of Indigenous Australian sports.

A theoretical approach that is related to ideas of continuity and hybridity, one that has been used in examinations of indigenous sporting experiences, is the theory that new practices (innovations) are diffused into the existing culture. In his study of Aborigines in cricket, Whimpress takes the theory of diffusion from sociology and redefines it to explain how a new cultural practice, such as colonial cricket, was introduced to the old cultures of Aborigines. As is the case with continuity, diffusion relies on understandings of meanings that are attached to certain practices. He takes from its sociological roots the idea that an innovation must be compatible with the existing values of a group for it to be integrated into the existing way of life. In identifying the distinct phases of acceptance, Whimpress also makes a relevant connection between important individuals and the introduction and acceptance of innovations into the old ways. He suggests that cricket came into indigenous cultures as 'innovations' that 'spread...to opinion leaders and from them by way of personal communication channels to their followers' (1999: 16). This method of tracing changes has been useful in my study of Wiradjuri communities, which includes influential community elder relationships. In particular, the idea of the Bidja, or leader, and certain influential outsiders, appears to support this explanation of how certain European sports were acquired by the Wiradjuri. Whimpress argues that the diffusion of innovations is 'a multi-layered theory which prompts questions at a range of levels and times' (1999: 18). This also fits with the idea of a culture being dynamic, a notion that is a foundation of the idea of continuity. Diffusions, then, offer a way of explaining how certain sports were taken up by the Wiradjuri while simultaneously considering continuity and hybridity of culture.

Bale and Sang's examination of Kenyan running considered continuity alongside ideas of 'geographical diffusion' of European or 'modern sport'. They argued that 'modern' or European sport had diffused into Kenyan cultures to the point that it 'replaced traditional folk-games of tribal Kenyan society' (1996: 69). Geographical diffusion or the movement of 'modern sport' allows European sports to be traced temporally and judgements to be made about whether continuity can be reasonably established between the past and present. Bale and Sang's judgement that Kenyan running was ultimately neither an example of continuity of traditional movement culture, nor an example of 'creolisation' or hybridity of British and Kenyan culture, is based predominately on observations of physical aspects of sport. However, they do not consider the possibility that meanings and values can be carried into the modern world in the adoption of relevant sports. American researcher Stephen Hardy has also used the terms continuity and long residuals when encouraging sports researchers to examine sport over a period of time to search out persistences (1996). He uses concepts such as 'dynamic' and 'continuities across time' that, he suggests, can be found in meanings as well as in observable actions or forms. Macdonald uses this concept of dynamic rather than static culture in studying Wiradjuri culture and Hardy argues that it should be used more often in sports history. This gives some support for the use of continuity as an appropriate framework to examine and explain the distinctly different culture or ways of playing and experiencing sport.

Continuity of culture as a concept relates to ideas about the way colonisers control the representation of colonised people. In Australia, controlling identity includes claims of discontinuity that support ideas about Indigenous cultures not being authentic. Continuity, then, is part of an alternative to the idea of discontinuity that some argue characterises Indigenous cultures in Australia. Continuity is therefore a part of the battle for control of identity. Discontinuity is a key component to the ways that difference is understood.

Words

Representations of difference matter in many seemingly small but important ways. All five of my children attend school in Cowra. They go to a school that June, Margaret, Mavis and Millie were once barred from. Two attend the high school that I dropped out of. This was the same school that Mavis quit because teachers sat her at the back of the classroom and ignored her. However, things have changed, segregation ended and there has been a genuine attempt at inclusion at the school in recent years. Still, it did not shock me to hear that a teacher at the school recently commented that he was 'a middle-aged white man' who did not 'have anything in common with the Aboriginal students'. Comments such as this raise questions about what people know about Indigenous Australians and how they come to know us.

The idea of deficit is closely linked to the teacher's comments. The sports discourse, which is central to the way that many learn about Indigenous Australian people and communities, is saturated with the language of deficit — sports stories that describe ghettos, that use the word community in inverted commas when referring to missions and reserves, and talk about people from them being 'hungry' and 'needy' and finding 'social acceptance' and 'upward social mobility' through sport. This language of deficit is common in but not limited to the sports discourse.

A 2007 essay from Noel Pearson demonstrates how the language of deficit can saturate what people say about us. In twenty-five pages he uses the words social chaos, erosion, misery, breakdown, dysfunction, violence, injured, withered, moral wreckage, abusers, self-harming, poverty, destructive, passive, and self-perpetuating. Pearson wrote about Indigenous people being disengaged, at the bottom, and being irresponsible, disadvantaged, wrongdoers and offenders, and wrote about the plight of damaged and demoralised, abject people (2007: 13–58). It is understandable that a non-Indigenous teacher might think he has nothing in common with Indigenous students given this type of representation. Pearson may be writing about extreme cases; however, for people with little background knowledge of our communities or limited personal experience with Indigenous Australians, it is a short step to attribute such negative representations to all.

Storytelling at Erambie is part of the community's oral history tradition. There is repetition and continuity. Questions are asked and listeners are expected to finish certain stories and help tell others. There are outright questions and even requests to write some things down. Photographs are read like books and young people were expected to be able to read them too. A lot of topics are covered from a vast repertoire. A ritualised tribal fight that happened years before not far from the mission is remembered. The value to be found in the continuing ritual through bare-knuckle fights is made clear. There is recounting of funny memories of childhood and the descriptions of a 'clever man' known to *bahloo* (kill) people. The *bidja* is remembered for leading the community through a transition from 'tribal part' into a new world and it is told that even he was wary of *buggenj* and *birricks*. The origins of the community are taught alongside family histories and connections to people and places. It is the history of a wonderful community, recorded with fond memories of dancing on the riverbank and modern dances in the corrugated iron huts on the mission.

Not all subjects are light. There were dark times under the government's Aborigines Welfare and Protection boards. Young people at Erambie learn about children being taken away long before that practice was labelled and written about in textbooks. I learned about it from the point of view of two child witnesses who watched it happen from a hiding place under a house. They watched their cousins marched out of a happy home and taken away in a big black car. Their fourteen-year-old sister, Mavis, watched from the yard where she positioned herself protectively between her siblings and the police while being a witness to what she described as evil. Children were warned to watch out for that black car as they walked into town to go to school.

Quite often the speaker places a hand on a young listener as they speak, as if certain topics require more than just listening to be really understood. Important stories about sharing as the essence of our culture are repeated endlessly. The best stories are about people and what they mean to our community. Lessons are histories and they are usually taught as biography. Mavis tells one such story about how she learnt about ambition when she was eleven years old. One day she read her cousin's name where it was written on their outhouse wall. Underneath it, someone had added: 'A man's ambition must be small to write his name on the [out]house wall', and Mavis went inside and asked her mum, 'what's ambition?' After scolding her husband and laughing at his joke, a mother taught her daughter about ambition. Mavis talks about happy times with parents and grandparents. Senior men and women remember homes filled with laughter and enjoyment.

My interest in history directed me to certain accomplished people who knew about history. Some of them themselves created history with their work in education, health, employment and human rights activism. There was of a member of the Order of Australia, a Member of the British Empire, published authors, university graduates including one Harvard graduate. All were inspired by charismatic and engaging teachers on the verandas and in the living rooms of Erambie's storytellers.

The teacher's comment can be read in a number of ways. One is consistent with the idea that people create places for other people as a way of ordering society. And they order it to their own advantage. The teacher who does not see in Koori students the attributes that made him successful puts himself in a different (and superior) place to them. He is a successful learner who contributes to society. If he has nothing in common with Koori kids, what does that say about them?

The language of deficit is relentless in representing Indigenous communities as places where inhuman behaviour occurs among people who have no values. With this in mind, Noel Pearson is right to argue for an approach to thinking about Aborigines that assumes a common human identity, a shared peoplehood. He is reminding outsiders that we have things in common, even though there are differences. This is important precisely because Indigenous Australian identities have historically been represented as different and inferior. However, an unintended consequence of the language that some use when describing our communities is that our identity is placed further away from — not closer to — a shared peoplehood. Negative language paints a picture of inferior and even inhuman communities.

Representations are important. It is important that people who talk and write about us consider the various ways their words are read. Indigenous Australians are more than the sum of our grievances. Our communities are not places of extreme cultural breakdown and loss.

For the senior men and women at Erambie there is no question that Wiradjuri ways of being continue. They make connections to the past when explaining much of what they see on the mission every day. There is a strong desire to see the 'old ways' continue. Mavis, Millie and Norma hope to see some form of integration for their grandchildren. They angrily reject assimilation when talking about their ambitions for their grandchildren. Listening to Mavis tell yarns about the past and discussing her hopes for her grandchildren, it is clear that she understands the importance of representations. Part of Mavis' hope for her grandchildren is that teachers understand that education is something to be shared. She is concerned that people learn about Indigenous communities as good places. She warned that, 'if the white man says, "do it my way", that's not going to work'. Mavis wants people to realise that 'you can't turn blacks into whites', and that 'we're not problems to be solved'. She hopes her grandchildren will be ambitious and 'go right through school and get on in life', but that they 'continue to be proud of what they are'.